Keys

to a Successful

YOUTH CHOIR
MINISTRY

John V. Link
Gerald Ware

CHURCH
STREET
PRESS

Nashville, Tennessee

ISBN 0-7673-3456-6 DP

Printed in the United States of America
Music Ministries Department
The Sunday School Board of the Southern Baptist Convention
127 Ninth Avenue, North
Nashville, Tennessee 37234

Editorial Personnel:
Jere V. Adams, Connie Powell,
René Holt, Deborah Hickerson
Graphic Designer: Wendell McGuirk

To order additional copies of this resource:
WRITE Customer Service Center,
127 Ninth Avenue North, Nashville, TN 37234-0113;
FAX order to (615) 251-5933;
PHONE 1-800-458-2772; or
E-MAIL to CustomerService@bssb.com.

Contents

Preface

The ageless Spiritual was approaching its final note. The 50-voice youth choir had built in dynamic intensity until the seams were about to burst! All eyes were on the conductor as he savored the sound to the very last second before bringing in the final downbeat. Finally, the choir moved into a well-rounded vowel and burst into six parts. The basses, firmly on the low G, acted as an anchor to keep the choir from flying away into regions unknown. Each part was placed so distinctly that a high overtone was heard reinforcing the lone soprano singing a high B. The entire choir was overwhelmed with the sound. Reluctantly, the director gave the cutoff. For the slightest second it seemed that angels were heard echoing the sound, not willing to let it die. There was silence. Then a wide smile spread among the rows of choir members as they realized what they had accomplished. They broke into an applause for lack of an audience. Cheers were heard and many eyes blinked back tears. Success never tasted sweeter!

I awoke with a jolt in the unfamiliar room. It seemed the choir's last chord was still ringing in my ears. As my heart raced, my senses began to clear. My spirit began to sink as I realized it was a dream—just an unobtainable, wild dream.

Unable to sleep again, I took a walk in the cool night air of Ridgecrest™ Baptist Conference Center. I thought of my own youth choir of 20 that struggled with three parts. Frustration set in, but it was eventually overcome with the thought of challenge. I set a goal to recreate that dream in reality. Whatever it took, I wanted that taste of success to be real!

It has been 15 years since that disturbing night on the Ridgecrest, North Carolina, campus. The journey has been long, with many pitfalls and disappointments, but there have also been successes. With the help of conferences, seminars, and the patient guidance of many wiser and more experienced youth choir directors, there have been 12 consecutive years of viable, motivated, and musical youth choirs. Through suggestions from others, trial and error, and time and effort, I have devised a pattern of success for my youth choirs.

As cowriters of this book, Gerald Ware and I come from different parts of the nation and minister to two different styles and sizes of congregations. Our approaches to the subject of youth choirs are therefore different at times, but our goals in ministry are the same. No two churches are exactly alike and no two choir programs can function the same way. Two ingredients, however, are irreplaceable: time and hard work. If you are hoping to find a quick fix for youth choir that will make your group an instant success, you don't need to read any further. On the other hand, if you plan to invest years of loving labor into the youth, you will find this book very helpful in harvesting a lifetime of rewards from youth choir.

John V. Link **(JL)**

In 1963, the Lord moved a choir director named John Gardner to First Baptist Church, Siloam Springs, Arkansas. I remember the first choir rehearsal when John stood before a group of 20 7th through 12th graders and presented his vision and ground rules for a successful choir. "Here's where we are, here's what I see we can be, and this is what it will take to get us there."

I was one of those 7th graders absorbing all this and, yes, I was a little intimidated by Mr. Gardner's dominant personality and strong focus. Could I really trust this guy? Could I accept him as my new choir director? I was unsure about this new director who was challenging us to be disciplined, focused, and willing to follow a long list of do's and don'ts. Well, I went home and talked to my folks, who said, "You **will** go to choir and you **will** give the new director a

chance!" (Parents have a way of saying just the right thing at the right time, don't they?)

It took a while to get to know and trust our new director, but in the coming years we would follow him all over the country. The more he challenged us, the more we liked it. I'll never forget our senior trip to Florida. On the way home we sang "The Lord Bless You and Keep You" at the 1969 Sugar Bowl football game (Tulane University in New Orleans), amid thousands of people from Arkansas and Georgia. Here I am, having come full circle and having missed only three choir tours since that 7th grade year.

Is it important for today's young people to be involved in youth choir? **You bet!** John Link and I will be sharing different keys that have worked for us in our ministry with youth choirs. We ask you to take those ideas that *will* work for you, adapt them to your individual situation, and unlock the *joy* and *excitement* of working with youth choirs. It won't be easy or come about overnight. There's no quick fix, but, oh, the satisfaction and personal rewards you will reap with the greatest people on this earth: our youth.

Thanks, John Gardner, for sharing your life with me and showing me the *joy* of music! I'm a by-product of your ministry and your ministry is ongoing through me.

Gerald Ware **(GW)**

Purpose: Why Have Youth Choirs?

(JL) Why have a youth choir? What are our motivations for taking the time and effort? Let's look at some less than desirable reasons.

• **Tradition.** Many churches have a rich heritage of youth choirs. In the 1960s, youth choirs flourished in unbelievable proportions as the baby boomers were hard at work living up to their name! Thinking back on past successes may make you feel good, but reminiscing about the good old days with the youth of the 90's will only convince them that you have no relevance to the here and now!

Tradition should be valued and respected, but it cannot be the only motivating force for youth choirs. The rapidly changing society in which we live calls for a constant reevaluation of why we do what we do.

• **Every youth should be in a choir.** Ideally, we want every young person in a youth choir. However, idealistic opinions can get hung out to dry from stormy situations caused by youth and parents. When the parents don't see the need or the young person has no desire to be there, why force all to be miserable and have a discipline problem on your hands? Realistically, every youth should have the opportunity to be in choir, but if not, don't feel like you're a failure.

• **They've got to have something to do.** This reason can be a flaw in the structure of your choir from the beginning. If choir is being used as a babysitting service for parents, then the youth will immediately have a negative view of choir. You will also have problems finding parental support and involvement. The sacrifice of time and effort to be in choir enhances the importance of the rehearsal. It's better to direct young people who attend because they've chosen to come and sing.

• **We have fun in youth choir!** Carefully explain that the reason we have choir is not to have fun! Choir should be fun, but when fun starts to drown out the real purpose, you must take a stand. Youth choir is hard work, for both the director and choir member. Youth must be urged to make a commitment of time and effort to the choir and to rally around specific goals. Any youth who comes to choir for pure fun learns quickly of a higher goal and calling. Don't worry: when the final results appear, they will have fun!

(GW) Then what is the purpose for youth choirs? Music is the greatest expression we Christians have for proclaiming our love for God; it is the most powerful means by which to share God's Word with others. Consider these thoughts:

• **Youth choir is an essential part of our church's youth ministry as we minister to the whole person.** Our membership is composed of youth from several different schools and cities in our area. Choir provides a platform on which they can come together for fellowship without competition.

• **Youth elected to officer positions take on responsibilities learning how to deal with people, delegate authority, and speak in public.** They learn that hard work will pay off.

• **Youth learn that sacrifice and commitment are needed in order to meet a goal, which in turn helps them mature in their decision-making process.**

• **Youth learn to develop the vocal, instrumental, and dramatic talents that God has given them.** It is our responsibility to develop and provide a vehicle through which youth learn how to share their faith through their musical and nonmusical talents.

• **Youth become more Christlike by taking on the spirit and heart of a servant.** Youth are high achievers and goal oriented. The reward we use for hard work is the choir tour we take at the end of each school year. By the time our

young people reach high school choir, they are seasoned travelers who

    a. have learned to pace themselves on tour;

    b. have developed and honed their varied talents and have learned how to share these before large groups of people, and

    c. are physically, spiritually, and emotionally ready to face most any situation they encounter.

    Through consistency, discipline, and excellence, our young people learn not only how to share their faith through music, but how to live life more abundantly by giving their best for the *One* who gave *His* all.

    • **Youth choir is an effective way to reach youth and influence them toward a godly lifestyle. (JL)** Push the youth choir to memorize music. This helps the members to sing out, stand erect, and be confident. However, the main reason for memorizing is to get godly lyrics into the brains of our youth! Remember the psalmist said, " Thy word have I hid in mine heart, that I might not sin against thee" (Ps. 119:11). Most lyrics are either Scripture or derived from Scripture. This will have an eternal effect on the youth. Here's an example:

    "You're the only Jesus some will ever see,
    And you're the only words of life some will ever read.
    So let them see in you the One in whom is all they'll ever need,
    'Cause you're the only Jesus some will ever see." [1]

This is not straight from the King James Version, but lyrics such as these challenge our youth to stand out from the crowd and live for Jesus. Nothing, except for Scripture memorization, can be as effective.

• **Youth choir is an effective way to create discipline in youth who come from an ever-increasing chaotic lifestyle.**

Music is a disciplined art. Youth must submit to some sort of authority, participate in some sort of uniform practice, and learn self-control to be successful in a choir setting. Whether they know it or not, choir is instilling basic principles of discipline in their lives, allowing them to effectively function in their world. Standing still, cooperating, following a request or instruction, working together for a common goal—these form a part of basic discipline that can be used in future endeavors.

• **Youth choir is an effective way to instill basic educational principles into the life of a youth.**

Surveys have shown that youth with a basic knowledge of music have increased cognitive capabilities and are better able to think and reason abstractly. Higher scores in math and sciences are also related to musical knowledge. These reasons alone should convince parents of the values of choir. Unfortunately, our public schools have drastically reduced funding for the arts, increasing the need for churches to take the lead in musically educating our young people. If we do not musically educate our teens while they are children, our task, in youth choir increase. However, it is very satisfying to see a youth who had no musical training accomplish the musical feat of singing in choir.

To summarize, youth choir is an effective way to:

1. spiritually reach and influence youth;

2. create a lifestyle of discipline; and

3. instill basic educational principles in the life of our youth.

If you choose to embrace this purpose in youth choir, everything you do must follow these guidelines. How you choose music, how you recruit members, how you conduct a rehearsal, how you discipline, how often and where you choose to perform, how you motivate your group, and your personal relationship with the individuals in choir—all should relate to your purpose. With this in mind, let's look at some suggestions for beginning a youth choir, and explore the keys to a successful one!

[1]Gordon Jensen, "You're the Only Jesus" (WORD MUSIC, ©1983). Used by permission.

Your Plan: Starting Youth Choir

(JL) What if you want to start a youth choir from scratch? Let's take a look at the ingredients you need to have a successful youth choir.

• **The Director**. Let's get personal! Are you ready to be a director? Do you have the planning skills and conducting techniques to lead a youth choir? Do you know about vowel placement and supported singing? Don't get discouraged and don't sell yourself short. There are numerous books, guides, and classes that can teach you what you need to know .

When you feel prepared and confident, the youth will reflect your abilities in their singing. Also, take advantage of conferences and workshops. The time spent in these pursuits will multiply your effectiveness in choir. First Corinthians 14:8 says, "For if the trumpet give an uncertain sound, who shall prepare himself to the battle?" You must be the trumpet for your youth choir. These young people depend upon your direction and guidance. Be prepared with the skills you need, and the youth will gladly follow.

There is much to be said about loving the youth and wanting to be with them. Love does cover many faults, and we need that emotional connection with the group, but don't substitute love for skills. Be the best you can be, then love them with your skills. They will respond.

Not only must you be prepared with skills for conducting and leading a choir, but you must also have a plan. Youth can spot unpreparedness when they walk in the door. A director must be ready and prepared before the rehearsal begins.

Have a plan for your rehearsal; have a strategy for your month of activities; have a goal for your year with the youth; have an objective to reach for the six years you have them in youth choir.

(GW) The youth will become a mirror image of the director through observing his work ethic and his spiritual and musical goals. Longevity is the key to keeping youth in choir as they feel secure, knowing that learning to trust, love, and follow someone without question takes time and lots of hard work.

• **The Accompanist**. (JL)
A good accompanist holds one of the keys to a successful youth choir. You must have someone who can confidently handle all the complex rhythms and syncopation in today's contemporary music. If the youth hear halting sounds from the keyboard, they will not sing out and will not enjoy the experience. *A youth choir can only go as far as its accompanist.*

Must the accompanist use a piano? With all the advances in modern keyboard sounds, it would be foolish to limit yourself to the keyboard. However, unless you have an electronic keyboard that reproduces the acoustic piano sound in a very convincing manner, the live piano sound may be better than other keyboards. The percussive feel of the piano and the overtones of the strings make the piano the best instrument for matching pitch. You may want to consider using other sounds to enhance the performance of a selection, but learning happens best on the piano.

What about taped accompaniments and sound tracks? While these may be useful in performance, the sound track is a lousy rehearsal tool. It doesn't teach the notes the choir sings, and it makes stopping to correct sound or technique nearly impossible. You tend to rehearse a selection in its

entirety; thus you become a slave to the sound track. You also have no control over interpretation of tempo and expression. Youth get bored easily, so do not present a piece twice in the exact same way.

(GW) Remember to use your young accompanists in Sunday School classes, nursing homes, for prelude music on Sunday evening, and children's choirs. A capable youth can be used to accompany junior high ensembles or to help in sectional rehearsal. **Grow your own!**

(JL) What if you can't find an accompanist with the skills you need? Pray! You can't leave God out of this! Our heavenly Father knows what we need and has an abundant supply of gifts. You will never have a need in dealing with youth that God can't meet in a wonderful way...if only you will pray about it. Sounds too simple? It may be, but it works!

• **The Youth**. Ah, yes! The key ingredient to having a youth choir is to have youth. You can't be a leader without followers, so how do you get the youth to show up? There was a time when all you had to do was announce that you were starting a choir and the youth would flock to it. That is no longer the case! Youth are inundated with multiple options on how to use what little time is theirs. You must

compete with these distractions with the only thing you have that youth don't. Look in the mirror: It's you. Personal contact is the key to involving youth in the activities in which you want them to engage.

There's a story of a young man who wanted to express his love for a young maiden. He wrote her a letter every day for an entire year. Sure enough, at the end of the year the young girl got married...to the postman! It's personal contact that does the trick. Putting a blurb in the bulletin or making an announcement in the service does little to attract the youth. A personal phone call or a visit outside the church building speaks volumes. Spend time being where the youth hang out. The fast-food restaurant after the Sunday evening service is a good place to

start. Let the youth see you in some role outside the church parameters. When they feel comfortable with who you are, they will listen to what you want to say.

Youth run in herds and are influenced by their designated leaders. Spend time identifying the "leaders of the pack" and concentrate your efforts on them. One youth can bring in as many as 10 others. Also, realize how important the boys are. Concentrate on getting to the right mix of boys, and the girls will follow. Hey folks, we didn't say it was pretty, but it does work.

(GW) If you do not have a leader in your youth group, then mold your youth into leaders through positive encouragement. More about this in Chapter 3.

• **The Music**. **(JL)** Detailed discussion will happen later, but when you are starting a youth choir, particular care must be given to the music you select. Our world is success driven and so are our youth! To begin a choir, you must choose music that will give youth a sense of immediate success. A four-part anthem given to a new youth choir of 15 will not reap immediate rewards. Try something familiar with two parts. After the choir is established, you can bring out the motets. On the other hand, don't bore them to death with music that is too simple. Singing unison with a sound track does not develop credibility that the youth are accomplishing anything.

Be aware of the age of your youth. Remember that junior high boys are going through a lot of changes and have very limited ranges. Find music that allows the boys to sing a unison melody in medium range and let the girls try harmony first. Then branch out with the boys singing a unison harmony. The junior high boys can also sing with the alto line, but don't expect this to be successful in the first rehearsal. Success, however small, breeds confidence, and confidence in the director allows him to branch out beyond mere beginnings.

(GW) If we only do musicals, we are shortchanging our young people. There is a time and place for musicals. Summer is a good time for a musical to keep youth choir going. A musical is usually two-part writing (occasionally three-part) and can be learned in a short period of time. But if we limit our youth to a steady diet of pop-style literature with tape track accompaniment and don't encourage them to sing challenging, quality literature, we are doing them a grave injustice. *Good quality literature teaches our youth how to sing by using good singing habits* (posture, breathing, and so forth). My junior high choir (7th-9th grades) closes its concerts with Tom Fettke's "The Majesty and Glory of Your Name" (all parts except low bass line). I tried taking it out of the program a few years ago and nearly had a revolt on my hands. Youth want to sing quality literature. They want to be challenged.

• **The Performance. (JL)** Presenting your music in public is an important step to success in a new youth choir. Singing music in choir without a goal of presenting it to someone will kill enthusiasm within a group. Give them a month to get a little confidence, then go for it. Remember: youth have the best listening audience they'll ever have...their parents! Encourage them about their presentation and set a goal to sing again soon. Be consistent and aim toward a time they will sing each week. Plan your songs and let them see a long-range goal. They will respond to your plans. When youth see that the goal in choir is to share a message from God with other people, you have taken a major step toward success.

• **Festivals. (GW)** Festivals are important to youth choir. Not only does the festival provide a stage for the choir to perform for other choirs, it:

a. can act as a catalyst for the director who is trying to get his non-performing youth choir off the ground;

b. reinforces what the director has been teaching through helpful comments made by the adjudicator;

c. encourages youth to draw their own opinions of good choral sound by observing other quality youth choirs in action. Inevitably, choirs will comment on how good one choir sang while critiquing poor posture, bad vowel placement, or crisp consonants of another choir.

If your association does not have a festival, talk with your state music director about forming a regional youth choir festival. Two years ago, my association discontinued youth choir festivals for lack of interest. I called several people in my area (even outside the association) that had youth choirs and suggested that we do our own thing. A date was set, adjudicators were secured, and each church was charged $25 to help cover the cost of adjudicators and other expenses. Five churches attended with 7 choirs performing for a total of 353 people. The next year, 11 churches participated with 16 singing groups and a total of 633 people. Of those youth attending, 76 were nonperforming young people from four churches that had just started a choir or wanted to observe to get their youth interested in starting a choir. The goal

in two years: 1,000 in attendance. *Ask me how I feels about the importance of choir festival!*

- **Enlistment**

❏ Print out your Sunday School roll and highlight those who were in choir last year.

❏ Start four to five weeks ahead of time and personally call the entire youth Sunday School roll.

❏ Assign youth (10–15 people) to make calls to the Sunday School roster and turn in the results of their calls on an appointed date.

❏ Have two mail outs ready to send to prospects two weeks before choir enrollment: one to send to those in choir last year; one to send to those not in choir. The letters should contain the same general information, but the slant of each letter will be different, depending on former choir membership.

❏ Keep a prospect file on those who visit choir or Sunday School so you can periodically contact them about choir.

❏ Promote choir in the church newsletter and bulletin.

❏ Put posters in Sunday School departments four to five weeks before the enrollment party.

❏ Make personal visits to youth Sunday School departments;

❏ Coordinate a slick mail out to your area code, choosing only households with children ranging in age from children's choir through youth in the upcoming choir year. (See Chapter 5.)

• **Choir Enrollment Party**
❏ Have parents coordinate food and soft drinks.

❏ Reserve an area for basketball and other activities. (I do this with my younger choir in order to give me time to voice each student.) Older choirs could probably go ahead and start singing the first day if the director is familiar with their voices.

❏ Show a video of last year's tour or display pictures, preferably by the registration table.

❏ Hand out a **Welcome** letter that explains choir rules, important fall dates, and discusses fundraisers and spring or summer tour.

❏ For younger choirs, use this time to start the voicing process.

❏ Have two or three older youth give testimonies on what choir has meant to them.

❏ Take pictures of youth joining choir and keep these in the roll book. This will help choir workers to know the names of youth. All this takes planning and hard work. Good luck!

Your Procedures: Keys to Success in Youth Choir

(JL) How long could you survive in a day without your keys? How would you lock your house, drive to work, or get inside your building or your office? It's amazing how dependent we are on our keys!

Keys indicate that there is some sort of barrier that needs to be accessed. Keys help you feel secure in what you are trying to accomplish. Welcome to the world of **keys** to a successful youth choir ministry. Unfortunately, there are no passkeys that will open up all the areas for effectiveness in youth

music. Like the keys in your pocket, there are a variety of situations to address, and each forms a distinctive pattern to unlock stages of success in youth choir. Success is not going to be easily attainable, but youth choir work is a rewarding field that has kept our ministry fresh and challenging throughout the years.

Let's open some doors on youth choir ministry!

The Key of Motivation: The Ignition Key

(JL) We call the first key the ignition key because without a motivated choir, you're not going to go anywhere. One of the great lessons in life is learning how to motivate people and get things done. Motivating youth can be a great challenge, but, once you get the ball rolling, nothing picks up steam like a motivated youth choir.

An image comes to mind of the old mule that was motivated with a carrot dangling from a stick in front of his face. Now we're not saying that youth are mules (although we've met some that would make a good argument for that), but we are saying that the motivational principle can still apply in youth choirs. Find some-thing that they really want to do and make that a goal in choir. Then, when they reach that goal, place something new in front of them. Keep their attention on a goal.

(GW) The following quote on motivation was introduced in a staff meeting and immediately applied to junior high choir: "People are motivated by achievement, by recognition of their efforts, by challenging work, by being made responsible, and by experiencing personal growth. People are demotivated by poor administration, weak supervision, bad working conditions, poor interpersonal relationships, and the absence of a feeling of status and security." [1]

A TYPICAL ONE-YEAR PLAN FOR CHOIR GOES LIKE THIS:

• **(JL)** The year begins in September with an enrollment campaign. Plans are laid before the group for the spring choir tour. Attendance requirements and obligations are discussed. Short-range goals are announced, such as performance dates, and Christmas music. The majority of choir music points toward choir tour.

• Choir tour takes place in the spring. On the following Sunday after tour, plans are made for a reward trip at the end of the school year. This can consist of a trip to a water park or amusement park. Something nonmusical is best, so the youth can see the director in another role. Attendance requirements are given for this trip, also.

• The week following our reward trip, we change gears and begin work on a summer musical. This time is more laid back than the other months, but it serves its purpose for allowing the group to present musicals. We never take the summer off!

• The week following our musical we review the year through video and pictures. Then we begin a new year the next week. There's always a new carrot to see!

• **(GW)** Our choir year begins the same week that school begins, usually two weeks before Labor Day. We voice all students, show a video of last summer's tour, have refreshments, discuss attendance requirements, have testimonials from selected upperclassmen, and so forth. We rehearse the following week and voice those who have not been voiced, either before, during, or after choir. By our third rehearsal, we are ready to send out letters to our Parent Support Group (See Chapter 6.) and vote on choir officers.

• We take a summer tour the first week in June and conclude with a home concert. Our tour lasts an average of seven to eight days—no longer with a young choir. Our high school choir takes their mission trip in the latter part of June; both choirs go to summer camp in July and do not meet again until choir enrollment in August. Youth and children's choirs enroll on the same day.

(JL) These are just some ways to get the ball rolling! Here are some other avenues for motivation:

• **Security**. An examination of youth's lives must take place to fully understand how to motivate them. Youth have been raised in a high-tech, ever-changing world. They are continually showered with highly sophisticated advertising campaigns and entertainment

venues. What do we have to compete with modern-day enticements?

Another factor in the lives of today's youth is the changing view of home and family. Many youth move each year or live with different parents. Through all of this they are searching for something they know will be there tomorrow, something they can depend on. With a lot of hard work, choir can be one of those things.

• **Tradition**. Security can be found in tradition within the youth choir program. The pitfalls of tradition were shared earlier, but there is a difference here. When youth experience their own traditions in life, rather than something that was done in another time or generation, they find needed security in their lives. This supports the idea of an annual choir tour, musical, or special presentation outside church services. When the youth know certain things will happen each year, they are motivated to be consistent in their attendance.

The most successful tradition for us has been an annual choir trip or tour. Each person works year-round to meet requirements set for eligibility. As these youth have grown up through the choir program, they have seen their older peers enjoy the benefits of a successful tour program and are now ready to do whatever it takes to have one of their own. (See Chapter 9 for a detailed discussion of choir tours.)

• **Goals**. Hand in hand with tradition comes shorter-range goals, such as a difficult piece of music or a performance date. This takes planning and challenging the youth to accomplish more than the norm. A large amount of choir success can be attributed to weekly presentations of the youth's music. If they know they are singing each week, they will be more likely to make choir a priority. For years the same question was asked each rehearsal, "Are we going to sing in the service tonight?" Now the question has changed to, "What are we going to sing tonight in the service?" Wandering aimlessly through a year singing anthems chosen at the last minute can be deadly for a youth choir.

(GW) Always set spiritual, emotional, numerical, and musical goals for the youth choir to achieve. By striving to reach attainable goals, the choir members will feel pride in their organization.

To help the youth reach their numerical goal, first set up fewer chairs than you know will be needed. It's always good to see extra chairs being brought in during rehearsal. A long-range goal (if you have the funds) is to tell the youth that you will pay for a percentage of their tour if they have 100 percent attendance in rehearsals and performances for the year. Parents will make sure they are on time for choir. You can even give varied choir tour discounts for 90 or 85 percent attendance. Naturally, you can take this as far as you want to

go. It's also fun to set short-term, attainable goals with rewards of a fun fellowship such as a pie in the director's face.

• **Variety. (JL)** This is an important key to motivation which is often overlooked. Young people are bombarded with media presentations that take them from outer space to inner thoughts. How can we expect to keep their interest if we always sing the same old songs in the same old way? Be original and spontaneous with your youth. If you're singing "Joshua Fit the Battle of Jericho," have them march seven times around the church while they sing it! Change rehearsal rooms from time to time. You may even consider an outside rehearsal during the summer. Before giving the cutoff for the last time on a certain piece, turn to the next selection. Before the youth have time to let down and start conversations among themselves, announce the next piece. In effect, you are "surfing" the musical selections of the rehearsal! This does wonders for behavioral problems and talkative members.

Lead the youth to want to attend choir rehearsal and see what's going on or what will happen next! Keep your rehearsals fresh and lively.

(GW) Catch your youth off guard. When you have an

extremely good rehearsal, tell them you have something important to share the following week. Conduct half a rehearsal and then remind the choir how proud you are of their efforts in putting their best into each rehearsal. After all this, dismiss the rest of rehearsal for a chocolate sundae feast which the parents have already prepared in the fellowship hall.

Change the room setup every six weeks or so by having all the girls sit on the same side and boys doing likewise. Have the rehearsal in another part of the building or completely turn your room setup to the opposite direction.

• **Organization. (JL)** Be organized enough in your planning to keep downtime to a minimum. Watch a youth "surf " the networks with a remote and you will see how precious a few seconds are. There is much downtime in passing out music during choir, so put all music in folders and in order.

• **Music**. Variety in music is also a must. Nothing puts a choir to sleep faster than singing three songs with the same style or tempo in a row! When planning your music for the year, divide the repertoire into sections of fast, slow, contemporary, traditional, spirituals, hymn arrangements, choruses—whatever divisions you can find. Then choose one song

from each section as you determine the order in which you plan to rehearse. This simple procedure will save long hours of frustration in choir! Variety in musical styles will be discussed later in the book.

(GW) At the beginning of the year choose music that the youth can prepare and perform quickly. (See Chapter 6.) Start with a rhythmic number in two-part, with some unison singing for strength, that they can feel good about performing. Remember: it's best **not** to sing if the choir is not ready. Always strive for **excellence**! Rhythmic beat and beauty of melodic line are good, but don't overlook the words. This is the reason why you sing: to share a meaningful message that relates to both the singer and the listener.

• **Accomplishment. (JL)** Motivation is also achieved during rehearsal when the youth can feel a unique sense of accomplishment. These special moments are times when the choir can feel goose bumps as they realize they have achieved something beyond what they thought possible. This may happen only once during a rehearsal, but it needs to happen. That one special moment can motivate better than any speech or pep talk. It is essential that the director plan his entire schedule around this idea. Look for those times when the choir sings that special chord with a unified vowel placement and it sounds so good that it hurts.

Sometimes an overtone will be heard or the choir will feel exhilarated from the sound and will want to try it again. It may arrive on the last note of a piece or could come in a grand crescendo or a diminutive pianissimo. You can even find special moments in extended silence after a well-timed cutoff. Wherever you can find them, apply them to each rehearsal. This is the time when the emotion of the piece takes over from the nuts and bolts of the musical score. When youth feel that special sense of accomplishment, they will come back.

Sometimes, however, that special moment just won't happen! No matter how hard you try, the choir just can't reach that point on a certain day. Then come to a point in the music and stop, clap your hands, and act like you've just heard the angels sing. Compliment them and have them try it again. Many times in getting them to listen to themselves, they will accomplish what they haven't been able to do before. You are dealing with many different personalities and self-esteems. They all need a pat on the back now and then. The psychological area is half the battle.

(GW) You can **never** compliment your young people enough.

They are starving for this type of attention.

• **Spirit**. **(JL)** You can't move from motivation without talking about the spiritual realm of the choir. It's a fact that spiritually mature youth are much easier to motivate. Convince your choir members of the value in sharing their faith through music. Go over texts and talk about what they want to convey in their voices, faces, and even bodies. Involve your youth in devotionals and Bible classes. You can't get them to truly sing from the heart if their souls are consistently shallow.

(GW) Your choir members need to know exactly what they are singing about. If your choir has not experienced worship through the song in rehearsal, it will be difficult to share the joy of the music with others. Why? They will be singing with a head knowledge and the heart won't follow. You must help them to learn not to sing music for music's sake, but make your ministry to your young people a stepping stone that makes them want to sing. (More in Chapter 3.)

[1] Ted W. Engstrom and Edward R. Dayton, *The Christian Leader's 60-Second Management Guide* (Waco: Word Books, 1984), 55.

The Key of Discipline: The House Key

(JL) We call this key the house key because through discipline comes the feeling of unity and family. Nothing can kill a youth choir faster than unbridled behavior. Discipline depends upon the capabilities and personality of the director. Some people are natural disciplinarians, while others easily become part of the gang. Wherever you are, take a good look at these guidelines and adapt them to your situation.

(GW) There is a fine line between being a friend to your youth and being a leader. Let's face it, most of our youth come to choir for fellowship. We need to be flexible and give them opportunities to laugh and talk; at the same time we need to appeal to their consciences to make rehearsal discipline a spiritual matter. If not, we

will waste precious time and precious talents. In whatever way you approach these sections on discipline, make sure you are consistent!

Friend or Foe?

(JL) Many directors go to extremes in being the easy, charming friend or the cold, insensitive metronome who cares for no one. Strike a middle ground with this idea. Be open and friendly, expose your mistakes and get a good laugh. Never be afraid to laugh with your choir or to even be laughed at in a good-natured way. Youth relate to open people who are not afraid to show a human side. Yet somehow, in the middle of all this, you need to have a separate attitude to take charge of the situation. The discipline buck stops here. The best suggestion is to videotape your rehearsal, then sit back and observe your discipline skills. (This works well for conducting skills also.) My choirs know both sides of my personality. I always tell them that they choose for themselves how I lead them by their own behavior. I can hug 'em or hang 'em; it's up to them.

Commander or Comrade?

Are you sometimes accused of being unsympathetic with the youth? To correct this, try to have a more open ear. Being understanding can cover a multitude of sins. Allow times to be lenient and open to change. Establish an honest, open rapport with the choir. Members don't care how much you know until they know how much you care! Also, spend time with the choir outside the rehearsal room. Some of your most effective times with youth can be at the ball field or the local fast-food restaurant. They need to see you in a role other than choir director. Without a healthy, happy relationship with your choir, little will be accomplished.

Director or Dictator?

Youth love to talk! They are social creatures who love to mingle and share. Channeling that energy into singing is truly a great challenge. You must be the direc-

tor and leader of the group. You must not allow chatter to overwhelm your goals. So should you ban all talking in the rehearsal room? One of the best ideas has been to establish acceptable times for talking. Stop your musical barrage for a moment and ask a question. Allow choir members to talk as a group about the meaning of a text or express opinions about a current event. Then let them know, without a shadow of doubt, that it is time to conclude the session and start singing again. Channel all their resources into singing. By establishing boundaries in which to talk, they will more readily accept the times when they must give you all of their attention. Whatever you do, establish a pattern and stick to it.

Is There a Purpose or Is It Just For Fun?

Emphasize your purpose for having choir and being at rehearsal. Every member should know that there is a job to accomplish. Praising God with song and leading in worship can be a great challenge. Make it perfectly clear that fun time for fun's sake is held outside the rehearsal room. We do have fun in choir, but that is not the purpose for choir. After this purpose is settled in their minds, choir members will often discipline themselves. It's really nice at times to have the disruptive person reproved by the members themselves. Peer pressure can do wonderful things!

No matter what you do, there always comes a time when you must handle a discipline problem. Here are some suggestions to follow:

• **Be sure to make the boundaries clear and visible**. There should be no excuse that the youth did not know the rules. Talk about the rules, post the rules, follow the rules yourself!

• **Be equally strict on everyone**. Don't be caught up in personalities and let one get away with actions that you would discipline others for. This includes male and female alike. Partiality toward one gender can cause a world of problems.

• **Be consistent**. If rules are worth having, they are worth upholding at all times. Remember: youth are looking for some sort of steadiness in their lives.

• **Take firm action**. Have specific actions for each discipline problem. Just yelling at the situation will do no good. Restrictions from performances, trips, or even choir rehearsals can be used for dealing with youth. However, once you build up a reputation for consistency and firm action, very few will challenge your guidelines.

• **Don't get emotionally involved**. Showing anger immediately throws a wall up between you and your youth. Mete out discipline in a controlled manner. Remember who's in charge!

• **Be loving and forgiving**. We base everything, including discipline, upon God's love and forgiveness. The consequences remain the same, but our forgiveness should be given freely. Remember that more than directing choir, you are shaping lives!

• **Meet personally with the one who is causing the problem**. You get nowhere by correcting a youth in public. Get the offender apart from the others, look him straight in the eye, assure him of your concern, then tell him of the consequences of his actions. Many long-term friendships have come out of meetings such as this.

• **Encourage the youth who behave well**. Always compliment your choir on everything from vocal sounds to how they sit in the chairs. Verbally reward the ones who are acting like model choir members. Encourage those who are doing their very best. Remember that many discipline problems derive from youth who simply want attention. Let them know that they can get attention through good behavior! Tell them as a group that you love them. Positive reinforcement works!

CHAPTER 3

The Key of Positive Strokes: The Hope Chest Key

(JL) I'll never forget the day "the box" came into my life! My wife, Rhonda, and I were setting up our first household. We were moving in the furniture she had acquired during her teenage years when a strange, ornate cedar box was placed at the foot of the bed. I was told that this was a hope chest—a box treasured by many young women as they grow through their teen years. It is filled with hopes for the future and remembrances of the past.

It is now 21 years later and I still cannot give you details about the contents of the box, but I can tell you what it does! Whenever Rhonda needs encouragement, or just a light moment in her life, she goes to this box and brings out her memories. We usually end up sitting on the bed in tears, thanking God for what He has accomplished in our lives. These positive strokes help us make it through some of the hard times in life. Don't we all need daily positive strokes in our life? The youth choir is no different! Gerald is going to share with us how to give your youth the weekly positive strokes they need.

(GW) I have worked with youth choirs for 20 years; 14 of those years were with junior high (7th–9th grade) choir. For some people, this age group can be the most difficult. Although some youth are withdrawn, most are hyper and extremely talkative. This age group is moving from glasses to contacts; braces are shining on the faces of many; boys are afraid to speak because of the "squeaking syndrome," and everyone has suddenly become so...mature! The junior high student is no longer a child but a young person trying to find himself while being pulled in many directions by responsibilities at school, church, and home. Pressures such as family divorce, teen suicide, drugs, alcohol, and peer acceptance bombard their young lives. The junior high years are important because this is when the foundation of young lives (morals, emotional and physical makeup, spiritual values, and perspectives on life) begin to solidify, and life-shaping choices are made. Most young people are having trouble figuring out who they really are while struggling with the external pressures of school, peers, and family.

I cannot address every problem and concern brought to the rehearsal, but I can be responsible to make the rehearsal setting a positive, secure, and safe environment.

Prechoir atmosphere. The rehearsal should take place in a well-lit room with bright colors, posters, and pictures on the walls. The room temperature should be adjusted, and music should be in the chairs. The order of music should be written on the chalkboard along with important announcements and a BIG *"Welcome to choir!"* The director should be available, along with adult helpers and choir officers, to greet and help introduce guests to other members. If there is a new member, the director needs to "voice" her before choir and place her between two strong singers in her section The librarian should make sure she has rehearsal music. Make sure everyone is greeted with a warm welcome, a smile, and a pat on the back.

Along with check-in lists, have these things:

• **New Member and Guest cards.**

• **Prayer Request Cards**. Prayer requests should be shared at the end of rehearsal. Use the card to make follow-up calls or write notes. If needed, the ministries chairman (choir officer) can make follow-up calls and send cards or flowers. Also, copy information for your youth minister. Keep prayer requests on file and check monthly with those making prayer requests to see how God has answered.

- **Braggin' Board**. Keep this on a clipboard (include space for name, grade/school, and reason for braggin'). Youth love to tell others about their winning goal, test grade, or contest win. Follow up with a note of congratulations. Again, make a copy of this list for the youth minister.

- **Birthdays**. At the end of choir rehearsal, recognize those with a birthday in the coming week. The ministry chairman can send a card or the director can make a call on the birthday

- **"New Member" and "Guest" buttons**. Help youth spot someone they need to know. Have older youth in each section sit with guests, help with music, and introduce them to youth around them.

- **Prayer Partner Sign–up**. I started this several years ago for anyone wanting me to call each week, listen to prayer needs, and share prayer time. This practice has established some meaningful relationships with youth and has led them to be more focused on what we're all about.

Choir Rehearsal. During rehearsal, single out a person who's doing a good job: one who is focused on the music, using good singing techniques (posture, breathing, well-focused tone), and

thank him at the end of the number. You might even stop the music abruptly, walk over to that person, bend down to his level, look him in the eye, and say, "Thanks, John. You demanded my attention by the way you were singing."

Another fun thing is to have the youth keep their mouths open after the cutoff and look at the persons on either side of them. Their immediate reaction will be to laugh, but this does help train choir members to have well-rounded vowel sounds with focused expressions on their faces. It also helps to break up an intense rehearsal with lighter moments of laughter.

It's good for your choir to see how they look when they sing. Videotape your choir's performance and let them see themselves as they check in at the following week's rehearsal. Give special emphasis to how the choir walks in, how they stand, the expressions on each face, whether the words are recognizable, and so forth. Youth have to be taught how to stand in front of others and to sell themselves. They will be their own best critics.

(JL) If you don't have video equipment, bring in a large mirror so the choir can look at themselves during a song. (This will not work for an entire rehearsal.) Let them look through the eyes of the listeners to see that it does make a difference.

(GW) At least once a month, use a codirector to direct the sopranos/altos/cambiatas while you direct the tenor/baritone/bass sections. (This is especially helpful for a choir of 50 or more.) This allows you to focus your attention on one particular section or person, break into a quick sectional to work on a couple of numbers, and give each section more personal attention for vocal placement, posture, and so forth.

During the last 15 minutes of rehearsal, have a parent call absentees to find out why they

were not in rehearsal, let them know they were missed, inform them of upcoming events, and let you know if there needs to be an immediate follow-up call. At the end of the rehearsal, share prayer requests and "Braggin' Board." Then introduce new members and guests, thank them for coming, and encourage the youth to get to know them. Use the word guest rather than visitor. Visitor implies "good to have you, but I know you won't be back." Using the term guest is a lot warmer and more inviting for a return next week: it says "you are always welcome."

Close with a devotional thought. Hand out a billfold-size piece of paper with a Scripture and positive thought on it to six or eight young people (at least two from each section). As you hand this out, call each youth **by name** (Use the photo taken at choir enrollment to reinforce the name with the face.) and express what she means to you and how that Scripture or thought comes alive through her actions. The youth look forward to this and may hold out their hands wanting you to acknowledge them. Does this mean anything to them? **You bet!**

Post Rehearsal. Call **all** absentees every week without fail to tell them how much they were missed. If any were sick, I instruct the ministries chairman to send a card. If you can't reach a youth after several days, send a handwritten note. If a youth misses more than two rehearsals in a row, call to see if she needs a ride or if there is any problem.

Each guest, and person bringing a guest, should receive a personal telephone call inviting her back (along with a follow-up letter).

I have three letters I send to guests and members who bring guests. (See Appendix.) By the third letter the focus is on enrolling the guest in choir and once again thanking the choir member for her leadership in bringing others to choir and church.

It's a good idea to have a monthly time to meet briefly with new members to go over choir attendance rules, dates, workdays, uniform information, and so forth. Include choir officers to introduce them and their areas of responsibility.

Another idea is to always carry a slip of paper in your pocket to jot down anything positive you see any of your youth doing. It doesn't take long to write a note, and it is *much appreciated*! Let your youth know they are *important*, *loved*, and *appreciated*! Above all, use a positive approach in dealing with this age young person. For some, it may be the only positive experience they have all day.

(JL) One other idea about keeping in touch with your youth:

try cyberspace! I recently asked my youth choir how many were on-line and over half of them had E-mail addresses. I suddenly had a new access to my youth that I never had dreamed of before— immediate access! Sending personal notes or even open messages to all the youth with computer modems gives you another way of keeping in contact with the choir. It will be many years before cyberspace takes the place of snail mail, but youth have already embraced this mode of communication. They think it's "cool" when Brother John sends them an E-mail!

This is also a great way to keep up with alumni who have gone to college. Nearly every college now has on-line access for their students. It's a lot cheaper than phone calls and letters. Some companies are now offering *free* E-mail to subscribers.

The Key of Music:
The Office Key

(JL) The office key is the key to the important business of choosing, ordering, and presenting music. The choice of music has a profound impact on the youth choir. Admittedly, there are varying opinions on what youth ought to sing. Just consider this another opinion.

Let's say you have one hundred anthems in a stack before you. How do you choose the best ones for your choir?

• **Text**. Before listening to any music, consider the text of the anthem. What does it say? Does it teach anything important? Is it doctrinally correct? A text that merely states "Amen, Selah, Glory, Glory" 14 times is not worth the time it takes to learn it! On the other hand, an anthem with archaic words requiring interpretation is

hardly worthwhile either. Consider the youth who learn the piece and the listener who hears it on a one-time, got-to-catch-it-all basis. Make selections based upon what the youth can learn and apply from the words. Take, for instance, the following text:

"In a world that's lost, in a world that's cold,
Who can make the difference?
Who restores the hope?
I know Jesus is the answer and Jesus is the way,
I will go, I will tell for I am not ashamed!" [1]

This text speaks in a straightforward manner to youth and challenges them to think about what is really lasting in this world. When the youth learn this anthem, they are challenged by the text to become better stewards of what they treasure.

If there are anthems with hard-to-understand texts, be sure to do a text study (devotionals are good opportunities for this) so the youth will know what they are singing. Since doing a text study on the old hymn "Come Thou Fount of Every Blessing," the youth have made this anthem one of their favorites. You can't put your heart into the music when your mind doesn't know what's going on.

• **Music**. After whittling the stack of one hundred anthems down to 60 on the basis of text, turn to the musical aspect. Again, without listening to the piece, look over the anthem's musicality. Check the tessitura of the voices, make sure rhythms make sense, and word emphases are well placed. Can your choir sing the anthem correctly on a musical basis? How about the difficult rhythms that pervade most anthems today? Always remember the capabilities of your choir. There's no need to order an eight-part anthem if your choir can barely keep three parts together. There are many good two-part, two equal-voice, and three-part anthems you can use. It's okay to challenge your group with harder music, but make your goals attainable. Well-written music will sound good in two parts or six parts.

• **Style**. Once you have about 30 anthems which have survived your textual and musical analysis, it's now time to listen to the music. You will naturally gravitate toward the style of music you enjoy most, but remember there are well-written anthems in all styles. Your main concern is to make sure the style fits the text. Youth lean toward more upbeat style music, but when sung correctly, well-written slower songs have always been my group's favorites.

How about different classifications of music? Can youth sing gospel hymns, contemporary Christian music, choruses, and the classics, yet still be happy and productive? "Yes!" Your repertoire should include all types of musical styles, even the ones that aren't your favorites. Youth are more adaptable to varying styles than adults. The key is finding good, solid anthems in all styles. There are many meaningful, well-written contemporary songs for youth choirs; be diligent and find them.

Among a few contemporary Christian groups, there is music which has been arranged in a more subtle setting and turned into anthems. Make sure these groups portray an exemplary lifestyle that you would want to promote through your choir.

Beyond contemporary music there is a myriad of other styles to choose from. Some hymn arrangements have been favorites with choirs and spirituals are readily accepted. Even down-home gospel sounds and classical styles are accepted when introduced correctly. Some of the classics can even be used in teaching part singing.

Keep up to date on new music styles. With our ever-changing world, it seems something new is always on the horizon of church music. Don't be a stick-in-the-mud and sing only those styles you like. Variety in music, as in the world, is the spice of life. In all these areas, keep in mind the ideals of text, musicality, and appropriate style.

However, don't consider these "rules" of music selection to be set in concrete. About 1 in every 15 songs can be "sugar sticks"; they may not be all that good for you, but they sure make you feel good! They may not always teach a lot or even have appropriate musicality, but they serve as relief valves for pent-up expressions. These are fun times with the choir, but remember: they can't survive on a diet that only consists of "sugar sticks." Be a well-balanced choir!

Finally, there is another music resource for the youth choir...YOU! Who better knows your choir's capabilities? With modern technology you can arrange or write your own song. Music notation systems on MIDI-interfaced computers were unheard of 10 years ago and unavailable to the general public until a few years ago. Now you have access to music notation systems which can print the music as you play! (I'm waiting for the computer that will write down what I hear in my head!) Keep up with the latest in music systems and, of course, get permission to use songs in arrangements.

(GW) Remember: if the music you choose does not fit the tessitura and age of the singer, if the music is nonchallenging, if the text has no meaning, or if the choir cannot feel pride in what they have just accomplished, you've got problems. *Good quality literature will teach your youth how to sing, keep them challenged, and give them a sense of accomplishment for a job well done. Your youth will learn the joy of singing through a variety of classical, gospel, and contemporary literature.*

There is abundant literature available which will fit your choir and your situation. The trick is finding it. You need to go through lots of literature either by listening to a choral club tape in your car or office or by reading. Tapes are good if piano skill is not your forte.

There are many ways to find literature.

• Join a choral club from Word, GlorySound, Jenson, J. W. Pepper, Cambiata Press, Genevox Music Group, to name a few. Try different publishers and see what fits your worship style and the age group for which you are choosing music. If you have a limited budget, choose your favorite three or four publishers. Alternate one packet every year with another publisher to keep up with other literature.

• The Baptist Sunday School Board has publications you certainly need to put on your list, such as *Celebrate choral music* and *Let There Be Praise*.

• *Youth Cue* magazine is an excellent source that lists, with each publication, anthems that have been used successfully by choirs in the festival atmosphere. (See Chapter 5.)

• *"Joyful, Joyful,"* (Hal Leonard Corp., #40326317), was one my youth loved from a contemporary movie. Listen to Christian radio, also.

• Go to your local junior high and high school choral depart-

ments and look through their libraries. You can find some excellent literature that choirs have sung in contests.

• Go to other churches in your area and look through their libraries.

• Swap ideas through the mail. Send a packet of music to three other ministers of music twice a year. You will always find one or two new tunes.

• Join your state's Baptist Men's singing group sponsored by your state convention's music department. Directors are always sharing ideas, besides enjoying good fellowship.

• Attend state music festivals. You can get suggestions for some good literature in two hours and enjoy hearing other youth choirs sing. If you're not already doing this, you need to.

• For a fee you can get publishers to send you their top 10 selling anthems, but this may not hit the age group you are looking for.

• Attend Music Week at Ridgecrest™ and Glorieta™ Conference Centers. You will always pick up some great ideas and new literature from the reading sessions there.

• Compose or arrange music for your own needs: you know your choir best.

• Host touring choirs in your church. There is usually something you can glean from the concert in either choral or instrumental numbers.

• Repeat quality literature every five or six years—one or two numbers that past groups have enjoyed singing. It's not a sin to repeat.

See the Appendix for a list of some of my all-time favorite anthems used with junior high, high school, and youth ensembles. Musicals were not mentioned because of the importance of teaching youth good quality litera-ture. If your youth choir can sing the listed literature well, they should be able to sing any musical.

Remember: whatever you do, challenge your young people to sing their **best**. There is a fine line between just singing well and doing your *best*! **Never accept the norm!**

[1]Dennis and Nan Allen, "I Am Not Ashamed" © Copyright 1997 Van Ness Press, Inc. (ASCAP). Distributed by Genevox (a div. of GMG), Nashville, TN 37234. Used by permission.

The Key of Education:
The Cabinet Key

(JL) This cabinet key will unlock endless resources that are the basic building blocks of success. There is a certain amount of education you can accomplish with the youth you have, but the most effective training comes when you start them out as children. This takes a good preschool and children's choir program. After 16 years at my church, a majority of the youth have been in an effective children's choir program which has taught them a basic love for music, as well as the rudiments of breathing, singing, and pronunciation. This started when they were children and has carried over into their teen years. It's not good enough to have a children's choir; it must be a thriving, educating, growing one. If you do not spend energies on your children's choirs,

then you are not preparing for your future youth choirs.

(GW) Look at any successful youth choir program, and you will find a thriving and well-organized children's choir program: one where strong emphasis is placed not only on the training of children but also on the training of leadership.

What is the secret to a successful graded choir program that feeds the lifeblood to your youth choir? Hard work, meticulous planning, and love for both children and worker. The time spent directing or codirecting the *Young Musician's* choirs will prove invaluable as you later direct these same children in junior high and high school choirs. What a joy to see boys and girls grow up in the program and to maintain contact with them throughout their 4th through 12th grade years. Again, consistency, discipline, and excellence pay off in attendance, rehearsal focus, and performance quality.

(JL) Beyond this, educate your present youth as much as possible. Take choir time to teach them. Use the songs you're singing and give practical applications to your lessons. **This takes planning!** Begin by developing a plan to teach one concept of good singing during each rehearsal. Look through your music before rehearsal and find a few spots that will bring out this concept. It may be a high note to teach the sopranos support or a fast passage in text to teach pronunciation. This procedure will not happen automatically or accidentally: you must plan beforehand. When the sopranos have just attempted to sing a note and failed, that is the most teachable time for youth. Give them something they can immediately apply to their lives!

(GW) Good singing habits don't just happen. The importance of good posture, breathing, vocal placement, vowel production, and clarity in consonants has to be reinforced at every rehearsal. Don't just talk about good habits: demonstrate them and let your choir physically experience what you mean. Have them put their hands on their throats, tense their muscles, and yawn. Once choir members have successfully done this, they will know exactly what you mean the next time you talk about a relaxed throat or a well-focused tone.

Always look for fresh and innovative ways to teach your youth choir to sing better. Here are suggestions on where to find new ideas in every area of your youth choir—from vocal production to touring. You can glean new ideas which you can apply to your situation.

• Regional Workshops. Combine the resources of several associations in the same area and bring together many people to lead in a one-day miniconference, with seven or eight people leading or discussing several topics in-depth. Call your state music office to see what training opportunities are available at the state level for your music leaders.

• Glorieta™ and Ridgecrest™ Music Weeks. This is a wonderful time to congregate with people of like interests to share ideas, sit in on reading sessions, attend classes on many different topics, and hear musicals presented for possible future use.

• *Youth Cue* magazine, published by Randy Edwards, First Baptist Church, Shreveport, Louisiana, is an invaluable resource that gleans ideas from other denominations as well as from Baptist youth choir directors.

• Join your state Baptist Men's singing group. You can pick up some good ideas during a snack break.

• *Video Magazine*, published by David Bolin, Colonial Hills Baptist Church, Cedar Hills, Texas.

• The Internet. Many churches and state offices are now developing their own websites. Check with your state office and develop your own addresses of people whose ideas you respect.

• Subscribe to The Baptist Sunday School Board music literature for children and youth. This will be your least expensive and most accessible resource.

• Form a citywide or statewide metro conference. Pool your financial resources and bring in a leader in a certain field to share techniques and philosophies you can apply to your situation.

• Keep up to date on books (past and present) to get ideas from different authors. Examples:

✔ *Professional Voice: The Science and Art of Clinical Care*, Robert T. Sataloff (New York: Raven Press Ltd., 1991);

✔ *Leading Youth Choirs*, edited by Jere Adams (Convention Press, 1988);

✔ *The Junior High Voice*, Dottie Ferrington, (Convention Press, 1982);

✔ *The Diagnosis and Correction of Vocal Faults*, James C. McKinney (Genevox Music Group: Nashville, TN, rev. 1994).

• Another resource is Menconi Ministries, P.O. Box 5008, San Marcos, CA 92069-1050 (write for more information), *Media Update*, a bimonthly newsletter about youth ministry which includes "Album Advice," an alternative listening resource for CDs and tapes. Al Menconi writes for *Church Musician Today*, published monthly by The Baptist Sunday School Board.

(JL) Never turn down an opportunity to teach or give voice lessons. Any time you invest effort into one of the youth, the entire choir receives the benefit.

There are many other ways to improve the musicality of your youth. Many churches are developing schools of music to educate their members. Some offer lessons in piano, voice, and other instruments. Others have chosen to give class instruction in a variety of areas or teach basic music rudiments during church-wide training classes. Find what works best in your situation and go for it!

(GW) A school of church music can add several people to your ministry and help train your people to better use their talents in your church. If you do not have a school of church music, you could encourage vocal and instrumental teachers to give their recitals in your facility or let them use your facility for their weekly studio lessons. You might ask the teacher to give free lessons to one or two of your students who do not have the financial resources, but show promise in voice or an instrument in exchange for use of your facility. (These lessons would need to be given during the time your facility is being used by other groups in your church to conserve your cost.) You could also ask the vocal or instrumental teacher to help you on an Easter or Christmas project free of charge.

Young singers are not encouraged to take voice lessons until the latter part of their high school years because of the tendency of the young singer to imitate the voice of the older, more mature voice. You can, however, encourage directors to teach the basics of good breathing, posture, and vocal production at an early age.

(JL) Another area to aid in musical growth is the development of a graded handbell program. When children become third graders, they have an opportunity to be involved in playing Choirchimes®. By the time junior high rolls around, they have graduated to handbells. The senior high bell group is one of the most advanced choirs in the system.

What does this have to do with youth choirs? The youth learn aspects of music in handbells that they don't usually touch upon in choir. Key signatures, time signatures, and rhythms have to be drilled into a bell ringer, while the normal choir member can miss these aspects and just learn by rote.

Anything that improves the musicality of your youth is worth a try. Do whatever it takes to musically educate your youth. The best way to have a successful youth choir is to **grow your own!**

The Key of Support: The Back Door Key

(JL) In addition to all the other emphases, there must be a nucleus of support from parents and church staff which we call the back door key. All of your best efforts cannot be successful without the support of many other people who believe in what you are doing.

•**Parents**. These folks should be the most influential people in the youth's lives. Communication with parents is vital to the success of your program. When the parents understand your purpose in choir, they will support what you do in teaching, leading, and disciplining. Have you ever had a parent ground a child from choir? It is obvious that this parent does not realize your purpose and does not understand the disciplines that you teach in choir. Make these things known to your youth's parents. Get them behind you or even in the game with you!

Parent meetings are a must when trying to organize a successful youth program. Plan ahead and give them detailed information about what you are doing with the youth. Talk about trips, rehearsal guidelines, performances, and discipline. Convince the parents of your genuine concern for their children, and they will support you with time, money, and their child's attendance. Parents are invaluable in planning and conducting special events for the group.

Keep in mind that these parents often have younger children that will one day be youth. Winning over one set of parents can help your choir for years to come. There was a young boy in my children's program who was a special delight. He had a great thirst for learning and enjoyed everything he did. His involvement in children's choirs gave him a great musical foundation. He soon became a youth and was involved in the choir. As I worked with the parents to involve this child in choir, I realized that he had five younger brothers. Since convincing these parents of the importance of the youth choir program, I have never had a youth choir without at least one brother in the group. All were musically gifted, and this family formed the nucleus of my tenor section for 15 years! Boy, am I glad that these parents were sold on youth choir! What you do now can have an effect on your choir for years to come.

(GW) How do you get so many youth involved in choir? What's your secret? These questions have been asked for years everywhere our junior high choir has toured. The secret is in getting parents involved in one activity rather than working two or three people to death doing many jobs. The more parental support, the more youth will be involved.

Years ago our youth choir organization adapted the following plan to our situation. At the conclusion of the first two weeks of enrollment, a letter is mailed to the parents asking them to be involved in our Parent Support Group, with a deadline response stated in the letter. (Note: Cochairpersons of PSG are enlisted before the letter is mailed, duties and goals for the year are discussed, and assignments are divided.) [See Sample Letter and Form 2 in the Appendix.] After all enrollment forms have been returned, PSG cochairpersons and the director meet to:

1. select a possible chairman for each committee.

2. assign PSG cochairpersons calling assignments to enlist chairmen for each committee.

3. make calling assignments in any area where more participation is needed (sometimes a personal call from the director is needed).

4. set a date to meet within a one-week period to finalize all chairman positions.

5. set a date to meet with PSG cochairpersons, committee chairmen, and director to discuss coordination of PSG with junior high choir officers.

6. Set a date to meet with all parents. Important: when you meet with parents, have health/permission forms, list of PSG committees (telephone numbers included), upcoming dates of special events for the choir, choir rules, and so forth ready to hand out. Also, it is good for the youth director to attend this meeting to show support for your program and possibly promote some upcoming events of his own to encourage parents to be involved in every aspect of their young person's life.

How do the PSG chairman, junior high officers (president and vice president) and PSG cochairman interact with each other? (See Appendix for Form 3.) How do other junior high choir officers interact with PSG? (See Appendix for Form 4.) The cochairmen meet with the director once a month for the first two months then bimonthly or quarterly, as needed. There is initial hard work, but you will be surprised how smoothly this structure will run when everyone knows to whom they are responsible and what is expected of them.

Getting parents involved still won't solve all your problems. Hard work, calling absentees, planning ahead, outreach, and loving your youth are essential elements. Our choir averages 100 members most years with 40 to 60 parents

involved in the PSG. But don't let these numbers scare you! The concept behind the planning for a large group is still relevant for the 20 to 30 voice choir. Simply adapt it to your needs.

(JL) When you see the forms in the Appendix which Gerald has developed, don't be overwhelmed! Just remember that we have had years to perfect this system. Gerald didn't start all of this at once! (You didn't, did you Gerald?) Think of these ideas as a cookbook rather than a to-do list. Pick out the best -sounding idea for your situation and use it in your choir. Then, for variety and enhancement, add something new each year. You have permission to copy the letters and put your choir's name at the top and yours at the bottom! Use what you can and save the rest. It's all great stuff!

Two other areas which are essential for a successful youth choir are the church staff and music teachers.

• **Church Staff**. The final key of support must come from your church staff! Planning and scheduling comes so much easier when your staff is committed to the idea of youth choirs. Particularly, you must have the support of your youth minister to make the choir part of the mainstream in young people's lives. Involve your youth minister in every part of your choir. If possible, have him sit in on rehearsals and sing along every now and then. Involve him in devotionals, retreats, choir tours–anything to help the youth see that choir is an important part of the youth ministry. You must be on the best of terms with your youth minister; his support can make or break a youth choir program.

Some churches don't have the luxury of having a youth minister; you may be playing a double role. That's both a blessing and a curse! Communication and support from the other staff members is vital in growing a youth choir. Their attitudes toward your work speak volumes to the people in the congregation. Educate your ministers on the importance of choir. Have the youth give testimonies during an evening service about what choir means to them. Use the choir in effective ways to enhance the minister's concerns, such as outreach and evangelism. Without their support, your choir will greatly suffer.

• **School Music Teachers**. Support from your local school music teachers will enhance your program. Spend time with them. Offer to help them in any possible way. Show them that you are interested in their program. Help them to see that, together, you can make more advances with the youth than apart. This can be difficult, especially if the teacher is not a Christian. You may want to try these suggestions.

◆ Offer to substitute for the teacher when he is out.

◆ Provide refreshments during summer band camp.

◆ Attend concerts the school presents.

◆ Invite the teacher to your special presentations.

◆ Give the teacher a schedule of choir activities well in advance.

◆ Offer your church facilitie for any program or event.

◆ Take a personal interest in the music teacher.

The Key of Problem Solving: The Toolbox Key

(JL) My father's occupation was a brick mason, but in reality, it was more involved than that. My father was, and is to this day, a problem solver. He has the gift of seeing a project to be done and visualizing the completed work. With his eyes on the finished project, he is able to overcome any obstacle that lies before him. When problems arise, he has the ability to find the quickest solution and know what tools are needed to accomplish the task. Many times while "on the job" with Dad, he would send me to the truck for a certain tool from the toolbox. I was always amazed at what he knew was in that box and how he used those tools to overcome problems. The toolbox would always seem to sprout forth a new tool when it was most needed.

I would like to think I inherited the trait of problem solving from my father. As I grew up, I realized how important it was to know what was in the toolbox and how to use it. Let's consider some potential problems in youth choir, then let's look at the choir director's toolbox and explore the ways to use those tools.

• **Singing with Support**. Youth today are heavily influenced by the music they hear. Unfortunately, there are not many popular singers with correct vocal skills. Singing with support is a major deficiency in youth choir and popular singers alike. This is a continual problem that you must work on every rehearsal. Don't give up! Youth choirs can sing with support.

Start with a familiar song your choir members know and love. Confidence is the foundation for supported singing. Pitch the song low enough that the choir can easily sing it. Raise the pitch (You may have to sing it a cappella.) and begin to discuss the problems they face. Talk about body posture, breathing, and diaphragm support. Give them a goal to reach and slowly stretch them to reach it. Leave the rehearsal with some sort of accomplishment.

Bring someone in to demonstrate supported singing. Make sure it is someone the youth love and respect. I have even brought people in to sing with the choir in rehearsal so the youth could get accustomed to the sound. Get as close to their age as possible with this "singer." You, yourself, should be able to produce the sound you want them to make, but it always helps to bring in another person of the opposite gender.

• **Breathiness**. This is the dreaded disease of all youth choirs ; it is a reflection of what they hear in other singers. The crucial point in singing without breathiness is the initiation of the tone. If the sound doesn't start right, it's almost impossible to correct. Vocalize a tone with the choir or section on a hard syllable (k's, t's, or l's); stay away from the soft consonants (h's, s's, or ch's).

Teach your choir the importance of the conservation of the breath. Also, the glottal stroke is a prime tool to combat breathiness (*ah* not *hah*, *ooh* not *who*, and *oh* not *ho*). When a proper glottal stroke is performed, the vocal cords are shut tightly. No air is escaping to cause breathiness. It's a start on correct tone for the youth. My kids love it when I start talking about their glottal strokes!

Some songs are more conducive to breathy singing than others. Sometimes a faster tempo will not give the youth time to produce the breathy tone. A cappella singing helps them hear their problems and correct them. As always, you must be able to mimic their sound and show them what you want done differently. If you sing breathy, it's a good bet your choir will too.

• **Singing Under Pitch**. Several factors contribute to singing off-key. The first culprit is the ear. Make sure your choir members can hear the pitches from the piano. Work on ear training if necessary. If the problem occurs with one or two people, make sure they are seated beside strong singers who stay on pitch.

If the choir has a problem with pitch in one certain spot in the song, try changing the vowel placement. Many instances of off-key singing can be cured with pure vowel sounds. For instance, if the choir sings too low on the word "come," they are most likely singing "c-uh-m" instead of "c-ah-m." You'll be amazed at the difference in a youth choir singing "ah" instead of "uh." This usually takes place on mid-range to low notes. Once they hear the correct sounds, they'll find it much easier to reproduce them.

Posture is often the culprit in singing under pitch. Make sure the youth are sitting straight up in their chairs (Some tall boys may actually not know how to do this.) with their shoulders back. Even if it doesn't help with pitch, they look better!

• **Vowel Placement**. Continuing the discussion of vowels, we must understand the accents of the singers. Neutralizing the northern or southern accent will do wonders for the choral sound. I'm always criticizing the group for "chewing" the vowels. The word "face" is not sung "faieece." Singing the purity of the vowel and pronouncing the preciseness of the consonant give great beauty to choral sound.

Vowel placements also help in singing high or low notes. Sing a nice bright "e" sound on a low note and then vocalize up a scale. If you don't modify the vowel to a neutral sound as you ascend, you'll break your neck (or someone else's ears). All vowel sounds should modify to the neutral "uh" when singing high notes. Likewise, all sound should be clear and bright when singing low

notes. Again, be able to reproduce these sounds yourself. The youth need an example to imitate.

• **Pronunciation**. The difference between a good choir and a great choir is the pronunciation. When people say they can hear every word sung, then let the choir know that they have accomplished the greatest vocal feat. Without the words, our singing is reduced to mere sound with no message. Stress this more than any other area.

First of all, pronunciation has to do with the choir's attitude. If they are "into" the song and wanting to communicate the message, they will go to extremes to pronounce the words. A youth slouching in his chair and thinking about something else will not pronounce words correctly, no matter how long you preach the techniques. Sell the song to the choir first, then they will sell it to the listeners.

Technically, the pronunciation of words comes from one part of the body: the lips. Getting youth to overcome inhibitions about their lips is a great victory. Most tend to be shy and slow about using their lips when singing. Vocalizations using the lips sometimes help. (Try a five-note scale ascending and descending using "Ma-Ma Made Me Mash My M and M's.)

If all else fails, take a text that you know well and write it on a chalkboard with just the vowels.

Then write it with just the consonants. This will demonstrate that vowels bring beauty, but consonants bring meaning.

_o _OU _ _o _
_ _a_ I _ea_?

D_ Y_ _ KN_W
WH_T _ M_ _N?

(Do you know what I mean?)

(GW) It's time for rehearsal, and you've got a very important concert coming up. The music is not memorized, and the choir is still chasing notes. What do you do? Skip the warm-up and vocalises? **Wrong...wrong...wrong!**

You should take the first five minutes (and more if you can) to warm the vocal instrument, to train the singer's ear through building triads and singing rounds, and to correct vocal problems such as pitch and intonation. There is an exercise which Jim Whitmire suggested in "Developing Choral Sound/ Repertoire," Chapter 6, *Leading Youth Choirs* (Nashville: Convention Press, 1988, 79). This exercise not only teaches interval recognition, but it also helps the singer to blend with other singers (use a circle formation) to solve intonation problems in unison singing.

Exercise 1:
Starting on a C Major scale, ascend and descend the scale.

Exercise 2:

Do—Do	One—One
Do—Re	One—Two
Do—Mi	One—Three
Do—Fa	One—Four
Do—Sol	One—Five
Do—La	One—Six
Do—Ti	One—Seven
Do—Do	One—One

If using the numerical exercise (Exercise 2), do not use eight at the top part of the scale This will produce an unacceptable spread of the vowel and focus of tone. Several good sources in vocal production were mentioned in Chapter 5. Refer to this list again. Choral music teachers in local schools are a good resource that many people overlook. The Texas State Music Teachers' Association published a great book on vocal exercises titled *Tried and Proven Choral Warmups*, Southern Music Company, #B-452, San Antonio, TX 78292. Contact your local elementary, junior high, or high school teachers for resource persons.

Football players and joggers have learned that in order to get the best performance from their muscles, they *must warm up!* Why should we as "vocal athletes" not do the same? If we are to "go the distance" by using vocal muscles the rest of our lives, *warming up at the beginning of rehearsal is a must!* Talking all day **will not** warm up the vocal instrument.

The Key of Outreach:
The Garage Door Key

(JL) I know this sounds strange, but when I think of reaching out to my neighborhood, I think of the garage door! You see, I live in one of those communities where the houses are placed on postage-stamp sized lots. The houses are no more than 25 feet apart, which makes it a necessity to have the garages on the front side of the house. Now, I'm not complaining. It only takes 15 minutes to mow the yard, and I have had some wonderful experiences sharing with neighbors I would not have known if they weren't only a few feet away. An interesting, unwritten code has developed in our community where the open garage door becomes the signal for community fellowship! All I have to do is open the garage door and folks come by to talk and share!

Unfortunately, reaching out into the community with your

youth choir is not this easy. It takes planning and organization to do an effective job of outreach. Gerald is our resident expert in this area, so he now has the floor!

(GW) We are commanded in Matthew 28:19-21 to go into all the world…to spread the Good News of Christ. How many of you are so caught up in the administrative part of your work that you have little time for the ministry side, such as hospital visitation, church visitation, personal Bible study, prayer? I spend time weekly scheduling concerts for choirs and ensembles, along with planning major trips for junior high choir and senior adult choirs. My women's ensemble is in much demand during the Christmas season. Too much of my time is consumed with follow-up calls plus mailing photos and biographical data, when I need to spend more time looking at the stack of publisher's packets on my piano, not to mention all my administrative tasks and time for personal growth.

Here's something I've applied to my senior adult choir that will go like clockwork, save you time, allow you to "plug-in" some of your community leaders (choir and nonchoir people) who can help your church reach beyond its walls, and open doors for your music ministry that you may not have thought of or had time to cultivate:

a. One person in each of your major music groups (adult choir, youth choir, and various ensembles) would be responsible to one person, such as a retired church member who has community connections. This person would act as a clearinghouse to coordinate outreach efforts.

b. Music committee—enlist several people for a community task force to dream, make contacts, and reach out to places you may not have thought about.

Program Chairman
- Talk with city hall and get names of all civic organizations, with addresses, contact persons, and so forth.
- Contact elementary schools about youth or children's bells,

instrumental groups, or vocal ensembles to perform in school assemblies or music classes.
- Get names and addresses of all nursing homes, hospital rehabilitation facilities, and senior centers in your area.

- Talk with city hall about dates for special citywide events such as Christmas, Thanksgiving, Easter, or patriotic events. There is usually a person in city hall who coordinates such events.
- Contact the mayor.
- Get names, addresses, and names of wardens in any correctional facility for youth, women, or men in your area.
- Enlist a photographer to take black-and-white glossy photos of all choirs or ensembles you could use in an area. Set a date for all groups to have their pictures made over a one-week period. Update your photos by October of each new choir year.

- Mail a cover letter and posters, with biographical information, to every listing that has been acquired.
- Follow up with selected organizations (depending on the time of year for civic functions, seasonal events, banquets in churches, and so forth.) with a telephone call within a two-week period after mailing the information to see if interest has been generated. (Note: If you have a quality recording of any of your groups, send this along also.
- Once interest has been determined (using **Program Information Guide** below):
  - ❏ Check church calendar for conflicting dates with youth or any other activity that relates to that age group.
  - ❏ Call director of group to see if group is available. If they're clear, let the minister of music know about the activity and the group involved.
  - ❏ Place date on church calendar through proper channels.
  - ❏ Reserve transportation and any equipment through proper channels.

Director

- Enlist services of a printer in the church, if applicable, to:
  - ❏ Print on good, but not too expensive, 8½-by-11 inch paper a photo of the group, with biographical informa-

tion underneath. List the contact person, along with a telephone number. To conserve cost, use both sides of the paper when you have multiple groups.
  - ❏ Print 50 to 100 8½-by-11 inch posters of each group, with a photo on poster-quality paper, with group name in bold letters under the picture, leaving room at the bottom to publicize concert time, date, and place.

Minister of Music and/or Program Director

- Send personal confirmation letter, picture of group (with return address on the reverse side), and five posters of the group to the concert site.
- Make sure the group director has someone from his group to take pictures (slides) of the concert to use in the next church slide show. It's very important for your church family to see what your ministry is doing. Our people are our most valuable resource aid in our ministry. You may have someone who has great organizational skills but lacks the gift of witnessing one-on-one. That person may be able to help get your ministry teams outside the church walls in areas you might not have considered (or had the time to think about).

This will make him feel he is part of the church's outreach ministry. It is wise for the program chairman and/or committee ministry team to meet with the minister of music quarterly to discuss open dates and upcoming concerts to keep the lines of communication open. It will take a lot of work to get this ministry off the ground the first year, but think of the lives that will be touched, the souls that will be saved, and the new members that will be brought into your church family that might not have been reached otherwise. Is it worth the effort? Yes! **The Program Information Guide** in the Appendix asks all the questions you would probably ask. Take this and adapt it to your different groups.

Once interest has been generated with any organization, the Program Chairman will need to follow the schedule of procedures. (Note: Long-distance calls will be made from the church.)

CHAPTER 9

The Key of Touring: The Master Key

(JL) The master key of success, one that opens all the other doors of effectiveness, is the concept of youth choir tours. If you sell yourself and the youth on the idea of choir tour, all the other challenges

will fall in line. It's not a "fix-all," but it does make all the other keys accessible.

Simply put, above all music presentations—pageants, camps, and rehearsals—choir tour is the best event of the year for youth choir!

Let's break this down into bite-size pieces suitable for easy digestion. This is not the only way it can be done, but this will work.

(GW) Every choir needs that "carrot" dangling in front of its members to keep them focused and to give them a goal to shoot for. Youth choir tour:

• provides an opportunity for the youngest singers to get away from home for the first time and start spreading their wings. They never come home the same person as they left.

• improves social skills through meeting many different people.

• provides a platform for youth to stand in front of a crowd and learn to share the gospel of Jesus

Christ through song, testimony, and drama.

• gives incentive for instrumentalists to play in an ensemble, bell choir, duet, or quintet. Also, if the instrumentalists are capable, they can be used to accompany the choir on selected numbers.

• allows those instrumentalists and vocalists opportunities to prepare music which can be performed in church services, Sunday School, Wednesday night prayer services, civic functions, nursing homes, and as preludes.

• teaches responsibility through job assignments. Youth are in charge of the tour, not the sponsor. If it succeeds or fails, it's on their shoulders.

• teaches youth discipline, not only in music preparation, but in having certain rules they must follow to go on tour and to not be sent home if those rules are not followed.

• teaches team concept–either we all do it or we don't do it at all. If individuals don't pull their weight, the whole group will suffer. I have replaced older youth with younger youth to head important committees. That is humbling and does teach a lesson.

• instills pride in the organization as the youth know their hard work has paid off. **Success breeds success!**

• teaches biblical truth through memorization that will remain in their hearts forever. When the tough times come, they will draw from their choir experience.

• teaches youth the concept, "it is better to give than it is to receive." They learn to have the heart of a servant.

To say that a choir tour is the only way to go would be limiting our ministry in many areas. Some ideas for alternative mission/choir tours will appear later in this chapter.

MUSIC

(JL) What style of music should you sing on choir tour? How about musicals? What works best? Our tour music is prepared between September and Spring (tour time), so the tour music becomes the songs we sing every Sunday evening for our own church. I **do not use musicals on tour because:**

• It limits the variety of the music. No musical contains the full span of musical styles. Most composers like to write in a particular style and do it well, but there is so much more you can do.

• Stage areas differ in each location. Most musicals require definite spacing for props and action. You cannot be guaranteed any certain space on tour. You must be flexible! I have presented concerts in churches with a thousand-seat sanctuary, some with one hundred, a food court in a mall, and the steps of a national monument.

• A certain time frame is needed. To be able to sing in some public places, you must have a limited program. Sometimes you must reach the listener with a message in the time it takes for them to walk by! Even some churches will only give you 10 minutes of a regularly scheduled service. Some musicals require several minutes to simply develop a story line.

• Sound and lighting restrictions. Most musicals require special perks in these areas. You restrict yourself to certain areas that have these needs available. I always try to leave on tour with the idea that everything I need I take with me, including risers and keyboards!

So what music do you use on tour? Choose 25 songs at the beginning of the year with a wide variety of themes and styles. Use contemporary, traditional, classical, hymn arrangements, spirituals, praise and worship, jazz, blues, and gospel styles. Include fast, slow, and medium tempos of many of these styles. Make your choir learn every one of the songs. (Remember: this is after you have culled the songs on the basis of text, music, and style.)

I tell the youth they have a right to reject a particular song only after they have learned it and mastered it. In all the years I have done this,

there has been only one song voted out! Usually, the ones they hated in the beginning were the ones they loved at the end. The difficult song they labor to learn becomes the one they most like to sing.

By the time spring arrives, you will know the songs that "ring their bell" and the songs that just won't work. Use all the "bell ringers" in your program for tour.

(GW) Make sure you have variety in the final product. I have always used anthem literature on tour, because good quality literature is the best way to teach quality singing. If the choir can master a difficult classical number or four-part anthem, then it can sing the socks off any musical, because members have learned how to read, how to sing, and how to produce a good choral sound with confidence and good stage presence. The heart of my program consists of 11 anthems (memorized), narratives and/or drama troupe, handbells, testimonies, and girls and mixed vocal ensembles. If time permits, I use a soloist or one or two people on an anthem singing different verses as solos; thus, encouraging the use of as many people as possible.

PROGRAM
(JL) After you have music selections for tour, arrange them in sections by themes. Then...pray!

Let the Holy Spirit lead you in developing a theme using one of the songs that will tie in all the others. This sounds sort of backwards, but it's about the only way you can do it within the time factors, styles, and variety. God has always come through with His songs and His theme for tour.

Our "Say So" tour was based on the anthem "Let the Redeemed of the Lord Say So" with the theme being "Let the Redeemed Say...He is Worthy of Praise...He is Our Salva-tion...He is our Provider...He is Coming Again...and We are His People."

Our "Joy" tour was based upon the song "That's Where the Joy Comes From" with the theme being "Joy Comes From... Praise...Obedience...Service...Heaven...and the Cross." It's really simple when you give it over to God!

How about drama or testimonies? Unless the testimonies are rehearsed and drilled, they can get out of hand and off course. Nothing kills a tour concert faster than a youth who rattles on about insignificant things (unless it's a director that does the same). My best success has come through one- to two-minute, lighthearted skits that emphasize each heading. This provides a break for both the choir and audience. It means more work for you, but it's worth it in the long run.

(GW) I hold auditions for tour soloists, narrators, and other special parts the last of April as we prepare for a June tour. (Note: I call on a former church member who is a wonderful writer to write one-paragraph narratives on selected anthems. These narratives are written in advance and used at the tryouts.) The youth sign a list stating their name, telephone number, title of number and composer. At the audition, I have an accompanist, tape and CD player, and the director of my girls ensemble. The next day I post a list outside the music office (depending on the number of people auditioning) showing date for rehearsal with tour accompanist and date for rehearsal with sound system—usually when the sound committee practices their setup for tour.

Prelude Music and Program Music

We use pianists, harp/violin duet (or other instrumental combination), brass/woodwind ensemble, or bells in this segment, usually starting 10-15 minutes prior to the service (depending on the number of young people). Of course, if there are too many to use in that time frame, I alternate nights for them to perform, with the oldest youth taking preference at the home concert. These people are chosen out of the auditions held the last of April.

SCHEDULING

(JL) This is the most time-consuming job of all, and my best advice on this subject is to start early! First, decide when to tour, how long to tour, and where you want to go. This can vary greatly depending on the time of year and the capability of your budget to fund it. I have traveled thousands of miles on some tours and hundreds on others. I even had a home tour, where we never left the state. The destination is not really vital as long as you package it well. Do have a destination in mind that has a major attraction to it. Present most of your concerts at churches within your destination points. Try to choose churches no bigger than yours or music min-

istries that could use your presentation as a springboard for their own youth choirs. The tour is not only for the benefit of the singers, but also for the aid of the churches in which you sing.

Don't forget about presenting concerts in areas other than churches: shopping malls, public parks, national monuments, beaches, college campuses–any of these, and more, offer great opportunities to sing. When the youth share in public, they grow more confident in their witness for Christ. These opportunities have always been a tour highlight for the youth.

Unfortunately, it is getting harder each year to present public performances as the government tries to control our witness to the public. Advanced communication can help, but the best advice I have to control this problem is to learn a few secular songs and Spirituals to sing during these times. We also try to talk to the audience after our performances and to share a witness.

Don't forget to schedule leisure time in the tour. A walk through the local park, zoo, mall, or tourist attraction is a great breather for the youth. Call the chamber of commerce in the city where you are going and tell them what you are doing. Every city has some interesting place to visit. Be sure to plan for any extra expense this may incur.

Communicate with the places where you are going to sing. Make sure there will be no surprises when you get there. Design a preparation form with all vital details on it and make sure everyone fills out the form. Disclose facts like what time you will arrive, how many singers are in the group, and if a meal is needed. Ask about dressing rooms, singing locations, piano availability, and bus parking. All this information saves precious time when you get there. Overcommunicate! Then you'll realize how much more you need to do for the next year.

(GW) I start scheduling my concert tour in October each year, usually heading in the opposite direction from the previous year. I make contact with churches in the area we are headed and ask the same question: "Would your church be willing to host a large junior high choir?" If we get past that, we move to the next question. I also share some idea of the number of girls, boys, men and women sponsors, and if any of the sponsors are married, to help them start planning early.

I inform the church of our needs, such as a meal, dressing areas with ironing boards and irons for the girls (close to the sanctuary), housing, if possible (though the guys have spent many nights in a church gym playing basketball, eating pizza, and watching videos), and breakfast the next morning.

I tell them we will have our own sound system (if needed) and bell tables with adjustable legs to fit over pews (in a tight situation).

I let them know that I will have publicity pictures, biographical information, and housing lists in their hands no less than five weeks before we leave for tour.

I then send a letter of confirmation (while it is fresh on my mind) with a detailed list of everything we talked about. Once the churches have been secured, it is time to work on tour publicity.

Tour Publicity

Each April we take tour pictures one afternoon, in uniform, at the conclusion of rehearsal. Usually, this is just the choir, but if you have any additional groups for which you want to send publicity photos, now is the time to take that picture. I send two black-and-white glossy photos, biographical material, housing list, and five posters (generic—no picture, with place for all information) with a cover letter, again detailing previous correspondence, cellular number to reach me while en route, and publicity suggestions.

Advertising the Concert
Radio
- Send information on the concert to public service directors of *all* radio stations in town. (See Appendix for 10-second and 30-second spots.)
- If the church has radio access in the worship service, utilize this valuable time.

Newspaper (See Appendix for sample letter.)
- Mail letter **no later** than one week prior to the date you want the article to appear in the newspaper.
- Most newspapers have a weekly religion section or community interest section. Mail a picture and needed information to the religion editor. (See Appendix for sample letter.) In larger cities there will usually be more than one newspaper. Enclose two dif-

ferent black-and-white glossies for each newspaper.

Posters (Send with these instructions.)
- Display three weeks prior to the concert.
- Display in places which will attract the most attention: church bulletin boards, stairwells, popular businesses, shopping areas, college campuses—BSU, junior high and high school music bulletin boards.

Handbills
This is probably one of the cheaper means of publicity, which can be printed on your own equipment or professionally—maybe by a printer in your church. Send to hosts with these instructions.
- Please distribute these in the immediate concert area.
- Two weeks prior to the concert, place handbills in the church bulletin as an insert and ask the congregation to give them to a neighbor or unchurched friend.
- Have students take several handbills with them to school and place them in the music area for students to pick up.
- Leave flyers at restaurants and other eating establishments, only after asking permission to do so.
- Mail letter and flyers to other churches in your city and association, making the concert a city-wide or associationwide concert.
- Carry flyers with you in your car

and ask permission to leave them with service station attendants, and so forth.

Church Announcements and Newsletter

• Include announcements in Sunday and Wednesday evening promotion three weeks prior to concert, with picture of choir, if you can.
• Three weeks prior to concert, include photo and pertinent information (who, what, when, where, and cost) in the church newsletter.
• Ask the pastor to personally promote the concert.

Television (See Appendix for sample letter.)

• Mail the enclosed information to the television stations in your area (including cable) to be run as public service announcements. This is free.
• If your church is on television, run information about upcoming concert under a picture of the choir.

Associational Missions Office

Your associational office should have a monthly or weekly paper that is mailed to each church in your association.

• Mail flyers to the associational office.
• Request that the concert be advertised in the associational paper.

Internet

More and more churches are putting their church on the Internet. If your church has this access, publicize the concert on your web page with a choir photograph and all other pertinent information.

TRAVELING

(JL) Unless your church is fortunate enough to have a tour bus, this is the most expensive item on tour and must be planned carefully. I suggest that your transportation be limited to one vehicle for transportation of the youth, depending, of course, on the size of your choir. The greatest benefit of tour is the unification of your choir. This is hard to accomplish when you travel in four separate vehicles. It is worth the money to have all youth combined into one vehicle. If more than one vehicle is necessary, create different travel groups for each vehicle each day to help youth become more unified, and prevent cliques. The travel time they spend together cannot be replaced.

Most of the regulations that I impose on tour takes place on the bus. The youth are not allowed to have personal listening devices or video games on the bus. Why? Because they sit down, plug in, and tune the world out. This rule causes them to read, talk, play games with each other, laugh, cry, fight—hey, it's all part of the tour experience. A funny thing happens about mid-way through the tour: They get bored and, out of desperation, they start talking to the adults! I have had more meaningful, soul-searching conversations with youth on tour buses than any other time in my ministry. We've had doctrinal problems cleared up, confession times with spiritual renewals, emotional problems unearthed, and even a salvation experience. I would not trade this time with any other experience we have on tour!

(GW) In touring with a large choir, I have my buses divided by grades, with the 7th graders on one bus (my bus) with some 8th graders, and the older group on another bus. I need to ride with the younger choir to provide information and to answer questions the other group does not need to hear. Touring by bus is a great way to get to know each other. Tour places people in a confined space for a week, and they have to talk. Many new friends are made.

I suggest you ask the bus company to (1) assign a driver who likes youth and has a lot of patience; and (2) make sure there is a CB radio on board and in any other vehicles following. Also, it is wise to carry a cellular telephone with you so you can be reached anytime during the trip, especially in case of emergency.

OVERNIGHT LODGING

(JL) This always seems to become the time of crisis on tour. Cost and the number of chaperons needed prohibit public lodging over the long haul. A hotel is not a pleasant place to be when you are in charge of the health and welfare of 10 to 15 rooms full of teenagers! Staying at a church facility is acceptable on certain terms, but I always try to keep just one gender at a time in the same building. Spending the night traveling on the bus is disastrous for young bodies and voices that need a place to stretch out. So, what's left?

Homes. The best choice of lodging is in the homes of the host church. Although this has its inherent problems, it can be a benefit for all involved. The key to this, again, is communication. Make sure you have enough housing, pairing up people to stay together. Never let anyone stay alone with a family.

(GW) One of the requirements we have before the housing list is sent to the host church is that if any of our youth plan on staying with a family friend or relative (other than someone at the host church), they will need a signed note from their parent saying this is OK, thus, releasing the church from any responsibility.

At the meeting before we go on tour, I provide information such as "Don't Be a Sponge" and "The Way We Want to Be Seen." This covers good manners, why you should make your bed, and so forth. Thank-you notes are stapled to our tour booklet and are collected on the morning of our departure. Each note has the youth's name on the outside. We tell our host families after our concert what time our youth are expected back at the church. We have a fine system for tardiness: $1 for the first minute and 50 cents every minute thereafter. We have very little problem with people being late.

(JL) Write a letter that the host church can send to their host families clearly stating what you expect of them. I make sure the youth are driven to the homes by adults and request a bedtime hour. Insist there be no visiting from other choir members, and request that video/cable viewing be limited. Not everyone follows these guidelines (especially the bedtime hour), but a valiant attempt is made to uphold them.

I ask the choir members to be on their best behavior, of course, and to use the time they have getting to know the hosts. They are requested to share a personal testimony with the family and to leave a thank-you note the next morn-

ing. Each youth has the phone number where I am staying, in case of emergencies.

(GW) Staying in homes can be some of the most memorable times for our youth as they meet many different people, stay in some fancy homes, eat a lot of food, or are lucky to get a glass of water. All these stories are fun to compare the next morning when the choir meets back at the church.

(JL) I am continually amazed at the youth who say this is their favorite part of tour. It gives them a chance to fellowship with other Christians, sometimes with different social and economic backgrounds from their own. They have a chance to share their faith with adults and other young people. Many friends are made, and some of the youth still write to them after many years. It allows the youth to branch out beyond their own world and to find other believers in Christ.

Hotel. (GW) One of the least pleasant experiences on tour can be staying in a hotel, but it can be done. I make hotel reservations early—with the names of four youth per room—requesting girls and guys be on separate floors with no outside doors on the ground floor. All accommodations must have inside doors. This gives me a little more control.

- Room keys are placed in separate envelopes with names of people staying in that room on the outside of the envelope. If we arrive at an amusement park earlier in the day, I will have the sponsor in charge of hotel assignments go on to the hotel, get the keys, and arrange them according to bus. I do this so we can hand out keys on the bus and give instructions over the bus public address system and not bother guests, since we usually arrive around 9:30-10:00 p.m.
- Youth are to be in their rooms 30 minutes after we arrive (ample time to check and see where everyone is, get their soft drinks and ice, and so forth). If I see we are going to be later, I purchase soft drinks in advance and allow the youth to only get ice for their drinks. Rooms are checked at specified times (announced), and if an individual is not in his or her room, a fine is levied.
- Telephones are turned off except in sponsor rooms.

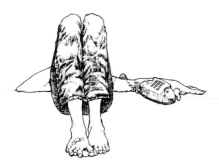

- I learned several years ago to tape the doors in several places, top and bottom, with a clear tape. If the tape is broken the next morning before a specified time, everyone in the room is fined and can possibly be sent home. We have a good talk about this before we leave. Our sponsors do patrol the halls for a certain length of time, but not all night.
- Wake-up calls are requested at the front desk for the following morning, and there is a room check at a designated time.
- Bags are to be at the bus at a designated time, and we leave at a designated time. Keys are collected by sponsors on each floor, and the director checks with the desk to see if any additional charges have accrued since the previous evening.

RULES

(JL) Bus rules have been discussed, but here are a few more guidelines. Modest dress is emphasized, along with the need not to offend another youth. Tardiness is dealt with quickly and efficiently. (No one wants to clean the bus or carry luggage.) Job assignments are given to each youth to perform when they reach a destination. Attitudes are checked constantly at devotional or sharing times.

No one goes anywhere alone! The welfare of the body of the choir is emphasized over the individual. Offenders are lovingly reprimanded, removed from concerts, or (as a last straw) sent home by bus. (The parents understand from the start that if this happens, they pay the bus fare!) Believe it or not, I keep rules to a minimum and very rarely have to enforce any of them. If they have made it through six months of choir rehearsals, they usually know how to behave.

Medical problems are always immediately revealed. There's nothing worse than a busload of sick youth who are passing on their woes at an alarming rate. Quarantine the sick ones in the front of the bus. **(Never leave home without a nurse as one of your chaperons!)**

(GW) We also have tour rules for our youth that, if broken, invoke a fine system. (Fine money is used to help pay the bus driver's gratuity at the end of the trip.) We have done quite well in years past.

Fines

1. Late for bus: $1 first minute and 50 cents every minute thereafter.
2. Failure to flip pin: 25 cents. One effective way to check roll is by a wooden clothespin attached to a string on a board. Each clothespin has the name of a youth choir member on red tape

on one side and green on the other. As each youth boards the bus, a roll call committee member flips his or her clothespin from red to green. If any pins are left red side up, then a check is made to locate the youth before the bus leaves.

3. Talking during setup: 50 cents every time you open your mouth. (Sponsors have pictures of all youth in their packets. This helps at times like this, as well as in getting to know the youth.)
4. Out of proper uniform for concert: 55 cents.
5. Quiet time on bus: 25 cents (Youth have their devotional time. After their devotions are over they can play games, listen to their CD's—with earplugs, write inner-bus mail, talk to each other by reading lips, or write notes to each other—they can't talk out loud).

6. Tobacco, drugs, or alcohol are not tolerated. There is an understanding that anyone caught will be sent home. (I have only sent one person home in my 20 years.)

These are not all of our rules or fines, but it gives you some idea of what can be done.

REQUIREMENTS

(JL) Remember that the purpose behind tour is improvement in attendance and quality of performance by the youth throughout the entire year. Thus, these requirements are made for the youth.

• **Attendance**. All choir members must establish an attendance record of 70 percent in all rehearsals and performances. (A separate record is kept for both.) This must be held as a standard for the youth. The entire purpose is destroyed when you fail to uphold this requirement. Set a cutoff date for new members to join. If the youth don't meet this requirement, there's always next year.

(GW) Attendance is discussed with the youth at the beginning of the year. We require them to attend 75 percent of all rehearsals. If they miss a rehearsal and performance, that counts double. Three tardies equal one absence. Those who join after Christmas must attend 90 percent of all rehearsals and performances; those joining April 1 are required to attend 100 percent of all rehearsals, performances, and an audition with choir officers, to see if they know their music.

• **Music Memorization**. **(JL)** All youth must learn and memorize all music before going on tour. A day-long retreat is scheduled just before tour to aid in memorizing and polishing the music. If you don't know, you don't go!

• **Personal Interview**. Each member is required to have a personal interview with the director. This provides opportunity to share the rules of tour face-to-face, talk about choir attitude, and have him share his personal testimony. This has been a special time throughout the years.

• **Finances**. Each choir member is asked to share in the expense of tour. This causes him to be more committed to the process. The amount is never high, and I do provide scholarships for those who really need help. The bulk of the expenses are channeled through

the music budget. Most of the monies from the youth go toward outfits and fuel expenses.

(GW) We have two workdays during the year to raise funds to offset the cost of tour: pancake day (50 percent profit) and car wash (80 percent profit for those

who take pledges and 50 percent profit for those who solicit donations only). We have a parents' meeting three weeks before tour when the youth and parent(s):

1. **Pay final tour costs.** They receive, prior to this time, the total amount due for tour based on the amount earned throughout the year. Any excess is applied to summer youth camp; anything beyond that goes into the "kitty" to help pay for any youth who has tried, but just can't pay all the tour costs, or to help pay the costs of a sponsor. (Important: If there is a young person who cannot pay for tour, but has made every effort to work in both fundraisers, has met attendance requirements, and so forth, a way is made for her to go on the tour.)

2. **Health/Permission forms** are completed for those who did not return a notarized form at the beginning of the year. Everyone on tour must complete a health/permission form before boarding the bus.

3. **What to Take and What Not to Take List/ Itinerary** (with daily schedule and important telephone numbers) and **The Way We Want to Be Seen** and **Don't Be a Sponge** sheet is distributed and discussed.

4. A **Fine System** sheet and **Disciplinary Rules** sheet (details of what it takes to be sent home, without a second chance, at parent's expense) is discussed thoroughly.

5. **Tour Departure Day**. What to do the day we leave is discussed: sign in, receive assignments (example: luggage crew has to report 15 minutes earlier than everyone else, every day), pick up thank-you cards—along with devotionals (which are placed in individual packets in alphabetical order at the sign-in table).

6. **Tour Assignments** sheet is distributed (We usually do this one week prior to parents' meeting.) and details discussed. Tour Assignments (Without going into detail)
   - Riser Crew
   - Sound Crew
   - Bell Crew
   - Drum/Synthesizer Crew
   - Truck-Loading Crew
   - Luggage Crew
   - Woodwind/Brass Crew
   - Bus Cleanup Crew
   - Church Cleanup Crew (in dressing areas)
   - Programs Crew
   - Program Pickup Crew
   - Dress Boxes Crew
   - Inter-Bus Mail Crew
   - Video for Tour Crew

The president and vice president are in charge of equally divided committees to make certain members are doing their job. Sponsors are advisors, not workers (with exception of the sound and video crew). If an older youth committee chairman is not doing his/her job, a replacement is made by the president after discussion with both president and vice president. Each crew assignment has detailed information about responsibilities—names of committee chairman and sponsor assigned to that committee. After the concert, those crews that have to get all equipment back on the bus are not dismissed until they see their equipment put on the bus.

OTHER DETAILS

Outfits. (JL) A decision must be made about what the choir is going to wear during performances. Depending on your resources, full performance outfits or matching shirts can be worn. It looks good to dress uniformly, and I believe they sing better. It is also nice to be dressed alike when you are out in public. You might consider purchasing a tour T-shirt. This keepsake can be bought and screened for $5 to $10 each. The T-shirt can have your tour theme on the back and even look dressy enough from the front to wear as a performance outfit. Expenses like this can be well worth the price.

Be original with what you screen on the shirts. For the "Say So" tour, we had a message "JUST SAY SO!" that brought many questions from passersby. (Remember the "Just Say No" drug campaigns?) Some choir members have kept their shirts for all six years–memorabilia they can put on their backs!

(GW) We have a uniform committee of parents and choir officers that choose the tour uniform at the first of the year. The youth are then given detailed information (what to wear and not to wear with the uniform, and so forth, along with a swatch of material for girls to enable them to pick the right material and guys to buy the right color slacks) and a cover letter with the date for completion. On our last tour we sang in a prison and decided to go with a choir T-shirt and bluejeans for that concert.

Tour booklets. (JL) A great addition is the tour booklet. It's not necessary, but it makes for many good memories. Develop a small booklet containing all the tour information, schedules, job assignments, devotional groups, quiet-time aids–all the important stuff. Then take time to do a little extra! Develop word search puzzles for destinations, song titles, or even the youth's names. Have a "guess who" page with unnamed chaperons' most embarrassing moments. Fill pages with funny statements or weird trivia. Leave space for hosts' addresses and autographs from other choir members.

Create a coupon system where the youth can tear out a coupon and use it on each other. For example: "This coupon entitles me to...your turn in the shower...have my luggage carried...an emergency bathroom pass...your place in line." This can produce hilarious results. Be creative!

Those little special touches can go a long way on tour. You don't have to do all these things on the first tour—just add one or two each year. Remember, you're developing a tradition for the youth to hold dear.

Sponsor Packets. (GW) Each year I put together a very detailed information packet for the tour sponsors. (If I were to add this to the book in complete detail, it would take up more pages than the book should contain.) After the meeting with parents and youth (three weeks before tour), I and the sponsors remain to discuss the packet. The packet includes (in detail):

- Itinerary
- Work Crew Assignments
- What to Wear (this is for each day's travel, such as when they can and cannot wear shorts, and so forth)
- The Way We Want to Be Seen
- Tour Family Group Assignments
- What to Take and What Not to Take List

- Fine System along with pictures of choir members
- Bus Assignments (who's riding which bus)
- Housing Assignments (along with who's allergic to cats or dogs) The sponsor in charge of housing will get a complete printout for each location for those who are staying with relatives or friends, along with a copy of the permission slip from the parent.
- Birthday List (who has a birthday on tour)
- Sponsor Assignments at theme park (Always assign them so there will be a sponsor with health/permission forms accessible in case of emergency.)
- Sponsor Jobs (committee assignments from work crews to fine collector and auctioneer of lost articles)
- List of nonchurch members and those who attend choir but have church membership elsewhere
- Copy of all narratives
- Sheet with names of everyone with narration, solos, special music part—if they have a special part, they are on this list
- All daily devotionals
- Where to look in the Bible
- Names of senior adults who adopted choir members and sponsors and their adoptees (include address of senior

adult to be able to write thank-you note to that person)
- Those getting off bus first (what to do when we get to church)
- Money breakdown (how much money each has been given per day for meals, and so forth)
- Letter of Introduction (detailed information on getting in touch with their youth committee chairman, when they are assigned to give a devotional, and so forth)
- Health/Permission Form (to be notarized)
- Driving Information (who is driving truck on which day with instructions about checking oil, filling gas tank the night before we leave, and so forth)

Sing whenever you can. (JL)
Don't ever miss an opportunity to sing. It may be a whole concert or just one song. It may be in a cathedral or in a pasture. It may be to hundreds or to no one at all. Every time you get off the bus, look for somewhere to sing.

We have sung in empty opera houses and cathedrals, restaurants and business establishments, roadside parks and downtown intersections. Every one of them has produced a memory for the youth. I still hear from some of the young adults about the time we sang in the zoo aquarium or empty megachurch. The youth love to sing, and they don't care when or for whom—they just want to sing.

I was convinced of this fact the year we visited the Coca-Cola Museum in Atlanta, Georgia. I had gone across the street to set up a concert in Underground Atlanta when the tour guide noticed everyone's shirts. The youth told him they were a choir and asked if he would like to hear them sing a song. He was delighted, so they sang a song right in front of the elevator inside the museum! And I wasn't even there to enjoy it! (I also thought it interesting that they chose to sing a Distler motet rather than one of their contemporary songs!)

Tour whatever you can. Don't miss an opportunity to visit nearby colleges and universities. The schools love for you to come and will sometimes even provide a meal. It helps if you have several juniors and seniors ready to choose a college. Take advantage of the opportunities to tour large megachurches of all denominations. Most youth have never seen a sanctuary which could house a football field. And I like to sing on their stages, even if there's no one to hear the song but us! Create memories; it will keep them coming back year after year.

We were in Fort Worth, Texas, one year and had a few extra hours before concert time. I decided to visit the Botanical Gardens in downtown Fort Worth to see the beautiful plaza of waterfalls located there. Pumping the youth up, I told them not to forget their cameras for a great "Kodak Moment." As we came into the plaza, we were surprised to find that the city had turned off the water to the park that week for cleaning the fountains! My "Kodak Moment" was nothing more than several acres of concrete! We sang a concert for ourselves and had a great time laughing at the fiasco. I've learned to call ahead! Even so, it is a tour memory still talked about today!

Senior adults love young people too. (GW) Several years ago, I started involving our senior adult choir in the lives of our junior high choir by asking them to "adopt" a young person for the tour. They would select a youth from a list containing each young person's name, address, telephone number, and school grade. They would then:

- call their adopted grandchild and let her know who they were and that they would be praying for her or write her.
- come to the next to last rehearsal before tour and observe rehearsal. These rehearsals are always productive

because everyone wants to do well for their "grandparent."

- arrive on the morning we leave to hug their young person, have prayer time, and give him a goodie bag. They may even make a banner to hold up while we drive away.
- bring a goodie bag for the bus trip. Some senior adults go overboard with this and even give money. (Note: Some will bake extra for those who do not receive a goodie bag for the bus.)
- send a letter along the way to greet them at the church or hotel. (An itinerary is given to adoptive grandparent.)

Adoptive grandparents are the guests of honor at our home concert with a section of pews reserved for them right in front of the choir. You should see the smiling faces of our senior adults as their kids perform and all the hugging after the concert.

GROUP SIZES

(JL) I hear the comments already: "I can't take a tour; my choir is not large enough!" I have toured with as few as 23 and as many as 65. To tell you the truth, I enjoyed the smaller tours more than the larger ones. Obtaining housing is easier, travel is simpler, and you can sing on almost any size stage. As long as the youth

know their music and sing out, size doesn't matter. Don't sell your group short!

SPECIAL TOURS

Every fourth or fifth year, I make a special effort for a unique tour. Every youth should have the opportunity to go on at least one of these. Take an extended tour, go to the beach, go out of the country (if you have the funding), or try a cheaper route: take a Mystery Tour!

Mystery tours are exactly what they say they are—a mystery! Plan your trip and all the details, but don't tell anyone where you're going! This is the hardest secret I've ever tried to keep, but the results are wonderful. Make sure something special happens on the tour, but it really doesn't have to be all that expensive. Give them an itinerary that has times, but no destinations or schedule. The youth love adventure and will go along with it. The parents need to voluntarily stay in the dark until you leave on tour. Leave behind all the details for the parents to pick up. This is not something you can do on the first tour, but when you have gained the choir's and parents' confidence, it works like a charm.

Do something unexpected and out of the ordinary. One year I happened upon some $15 one-way plane flights to a nearby city. With special sworn-to-secret permission from the parents, we got aboard an old rattletrap bus to start tour. The youth were horrified until we pulled into the airport! Many had never flown before. The tour bus met us at the destination city's airport, and then we had a rather usual tour. The youth have never stopped talking about it. And they show up every year to find out what is going to happen next!

(GW) I mentioned earlier that our high school/college choir takes a mission/choir tour every year. They usually sing anthem literature, but have used a musical, also. Here are some ideas for alternative tours:

• If you are low in attendance after having graduated a large group of people, have your youth learn a children's musical, make the set, dress like children, and make a tour of several children's homes or children's hospitals around the state.

• Every Christmas our youth choir travels to Texas state correctional centers. They sing five or six concerts in a three to four day span. This is my daughter's favorite tour because the inmates are so appreciative, and the choir has seen many people make professions of faith.

• Combine with other denominational churches in your city and take a tour to Methodist,

Catholic, Presbyterian, and other churches with literature chosen by each director.

• Several years ago, a Dallas youth choir took a train trip to Chicago and presented a musical in a low income area with good results. You could call this a "Whistle Stop" tour.

• Visit Baptist children's comes in different states. Go prepared to stay a couple of days in one city, spending time with the young people, conducting Vacation Bible Schools or sports clinics. Present your concert the evening of the second day to a group of people you now know.

• Go to an inner-city church to do construction work, serve food in a homeless shelter, canvas the immediate area around the church to enroll people in the church, and distribute information about your concert. End your time there with a concert or conduct revival services in the evening with youth taking charge of the service.

• Our youth take a tour every summer and lead sports slinics with coaches from area schools and visiting sports figures. This involves our youth in everything from Backyard Bible Clubs to tennis, soccer, baseball, and basketball. The gospel is presented at each sports event, concluding on Friday night with an awards presentation and a choir concert. An invitation is given at the end of the concert.

- Go to Indian reservations to conduct Backyard Bible Clubs and do construction,if needed.
- If you do not have enough in your church to take a tour, think about combining choirs from your associational or regional youth choir festival. Choose a central church to act as host for two or three rehearsals. Each of the churches would have input into the tour music. Also, if one church has a brass ensemble, a handbell group, or a vocal ensemble, let them perform. Allow each director to have responsibility for different parts of the program. Remember: the more people going on a tour, the less the cost will be.

- Mystery tour is a great idea (already mentioned).
- If you have divided your junior high and senior high choirs, you might want to (about every five years) combine the choir in a Ridgecrest™ or Glorieta™-type format (each choir singing three or four selections separately and combining on four numbers), touring to Glorieta™ or Ridgecrest™ for Centrifuge. It can provide variety and vocal strength to the concert. Breaking away from the traditional choir tour every three years will give the youth another view of ministry and how they can use their other God-given talents to spread the gospel.

As stated already, "Do something unexpected. **Be creative!**"

CHAPTER 10

The Key of Testimonials: The Trunk Key

(JL) Most cars today have a trunk of some sort. It is not essential to the workings of a car and you may rarely use it, but when trouble comes or you need extra space, it always comes in handy. Found within the trunk is an important tool for emergencies: the jack. It holds up your car while repairs are being made. The trunk key to youth choirs are testimonials from the youth. You don't exist for their approval or encouragement, but sometimes it sure helps. I asked several of my youth who have been involved in choir through the years to share a word about how important choir was to them. I hope this serves as a support for you when things aren't going just right. It sure helps me!

Once a year, usually during the Christmas break, we have a fellowship in our home for all of our former youth choir members. They have a wonderful time singing through their old songs, reminiscing about choir, and telling tall tales about their favorite tours. They are always so grateful for this time of fellowship, but I really don't do it for them! As I sit by and hear their hearts, feel their love for the songs they sing, and revisit the precious memories they have of choir, all the wounds and fatigue of the past year melt away. I am renewed with a determination to make a new generation of youth choir members who love singing for God as much as these who walk out my door.

Listen to stories of youth choirs past as told by the youth:

Bryan

"Youth Choir was special to me because I grew up in church choirs and really enjoyed singing. I will admit, I not only came to choir to sing, but to see my friends and to have the fellowship that goes along with singing. Each rehearsal was planned down to the minute, and each member had a folder with the music already in it. How much easier could it be?

"Being involved in the annual choir tours and summer musicals was a great motivator to stay involved, as well as a break from doing the normal rehearsal and Sunday night singing. We visited many churches on many tours, and it was great to have the opportunity to share our music with other people outside our church.

"Looking back, the friendships, blessings, and joys of youth choir cannot be described in one word. Being able to share God's love through music was the best part of all."

(Bryan is now in his mid-20s and has responsibilities in our audio/visual ministry. He also teaches in the Young Musicians choir where he was once a member!)

Matt

"Two things readily come to mind when I remember my days in

youth choir. The first is the fact that such vivid memories were created. Within my mind I carry moments and events that I have been hard-pressed to duplicate in other arenas of ministry and public service. Even though I am now in my postcollege years, I still remember several things from my first year in youth choir—and not just the special trips we took. Much of the fun and camaraderie culminated in the rehearsals. The music was our common ground. It was the reason we were there, and it is what bound us together as a group.

"The second special thing I remember about choir is the music. There are some songs we sang 10 years ago that I still know today. Youth choir is where I learned to understand what music is and how to read it. It is also where I learned to praise my heavenly Father and help others to worship Him as well. Music is a powerful tool, no matter what the style. The music we learned will remain with me no matter what."

(Matt is now heavily involved in our youth program through the art of video and works in the audio ministry as well as working with our junior high choir. Do you see a pattern?)

Cindy

"I first got involved in youth choirs when a friend asked me to come to rehearsal. 'But I can't sing,' I said. She said, 'It doesn't matter, just come on—you'll like it!' So I did go to choir and, before I knew it, I couldn't quit coming. Because it was a group setting, I had a chance to sing without standing out. Actually, this is where I began to enjoy singing. I was taught how to sing correctly without being picked on.

"But, more important than learning how to sing, I learned why to sing. I learned that there is more to singing than sounding pretty. It's the meaning behind the words you sing. It was in youth choir that I developed a love for music and an understanding of what an effective witnessing tool music could be. Because of all the choir tours, I learned how much music can minister to others as well as myself.

"Finally, I have to say that youth choir kept me going through those difficult years. Because of the lack of a constant youth minister, having youth choir gave me a reason to come to church on Sunday evenings. There were many times when I would have dropped out of church had I not had choir. Choir was the glue that held me together!"

(Cindy came to church even when her parents chose not to be a part of our fellowship. After graduating from college, she served for two years as a Journeyman in Amman, Jordan. She has since returned to the states and is now on my music staff!)

Kay

"It wasn't easy to put my finger on what made choir so special to me. It was just hard to imagine growing up without being in choir all the time. I still have to stop and listen to any choir music I hear being sung. It brings back a lot of memories! To me, the most important thing about choir was the feeling of accomplishment. As a teenager, there aren't many things you can do that make you feel part of a group effort and allow you to see and hear the results. Hours of practice, singing the same part over and over, listening to some other section sing their hard parts over and over, feeling you'll never pull it all together—and then comes the first time everybody really nails it. There is always a silence in the room after that happens, when everybody is thinking, Wow. We did it. It sounded great! Then comes the feeling that makes choir addictive: I was part of that.

"Next to that, the best thing about choir is the feeling of family. It's impossible not to become close to people you work so hard with and create something beautiful with. All of my best friends came from choir, and I felt most at home there. Even after I left for college, I would seek out the choir first when I came back to my home church because I knew those were the people who would remember me best and would be happy to see me. There was always a seat for me, too, if I wanted to join in that day.

"Lastly, choir was just plain FUN. We did everything—musicals, festivals, tours–and it was all a blast. We could just relax and be ourselves around each other, and we always had a good time. To me, tours were always best. Traveling around, the long bus trips, and singing together wherever we went—not only in churches, but in amusement parks, restaurants, and people's homes where we stayed. We got some weird looks, but it was fun."

(Kay was a National Merit Scholarship Finalist and now serves as an interpreter for the deaf in Virginia public schools.)

Now listen as the "youth choir of today" tells why choir has become so special to them.

Rachel

"I began singing in choir when I was in the second grade. I can remember all my teachers and most of the songs we sang, but, most of all, I remember being amazed when the senior high choir would sing in church. They made a recording once, and I knew every word on the tape! I couldn't wait to sing with them and to go on choir tour. Eventually, my turn came to be in senior high choir. I am now looking forward to going on my third choir tour, and I love it. Choir practice is honestly my favorite hour of the week. Besides loving to sing, I love to worship. Choir is my best time of worship. The songs go with me throughout the week, and it is amazing how often the youth of my church sing choir songs outside of practice. In choir, we truly obey the command of the Psalms to 'sing praise unto the Lord.' "

(Rachel was a year old when I started the first youth choir here at the church. She is now a junior in high school and, as you can tell, is a great promoter of senior high choir. Her love for music began in children's choirs and will hopefully continue all her life. She also has a leadership position in her school Christian organization.)

Jeff

"I have been part of senior high choir for two years now and, Wow!, do I have a testimony about my experiences. I guess it really begins with me going to children's choirs when I was little. I never really liked choirs until I reached senior high choir. Now you need to understand something. When you reach senior high choir, it can mean one of two things: It can mean 'YES, I have finally made it to the senior high choir!' or it can mean 'YES, I am almost done with choir!' So, either way, the kids are excited about something. I bet you will never guess where I was when it came to that. Yep, I was in the group that hated choir and no one was going to make me like it! I was not a rebellious kid, I just didn't like singing.

"I was not quite ready for what was to come next. Brother John was the guy all the teens liked, but as far as I was concerned, we were not going to get along because we had one major conflict: I hated to sing and, well, he was the choir director. I was very unhappy in choir and made no major effort to hide my unhappiness.

"Why did I continue to go? Well, my mom loved choir so much that she thought I should also love and support choir. So, reluctantly, I went to choir. This went on for several weeks until our choir really started to sound good. Each week we got better and better until it was just a few weeks before choir tour. I started to actually get excited about choir! Finally it was time...**choir tour**! Something happened at the first place we stopped on our tour. I

was having an awesome time. I found myself singing louder and louder. I loved it. We sounded great! There were times I would stop singing and think, Wow, I'm a part of all this! Then I would start singing again, but louder and with a large smile on my face. This went on and on and I loved it more each stop we made on the tour. I loved being part of something so awesome.

"You see, I can barely carry a tune in a bucket, but in a choir I'm covered by all the others that can sing and it sounds awesome. We feed off each other's joy. I guess what I am saying is that you don't have to be able to sing great, you just need to be willing to give it a chance. Just do your best and you will have an awesome choir!"

(This was one of those pleasant surprises that make those long hours of rehearsal worthwhile. Jeff could have been a discipline problem and out the door after a few weeks, had it not been for his parents. They deserve the credit for this catch! Remember that those who oppose choir the most will support it the best, once they have been sold on what you are doing.)

(GW) There is benefit to longevity in a church. Over the last 14 years in my present field of service, I have seen hundreds of young people go through choir whom I have helped raise, nurture in God's love, and now see coming back to their home church in areas of ministry. It's an honor to be asked to perform the wedding of a former "kid," to be called late at night by a young man or woman needing counseling, to have a young man, who is an aspiring writer, come to your house late at night wanting you to look at a manuscript and to offer comments about his hard work (with encouragement), to have college students send you their addresses and telephone numbers, knowing that they need to talk to you, or to have a house full of college students (four years after junior high choir) come to your house to watch a video and eat you out of house and home. These are just a few of the wonderful experiences reinforcing the value of longevity—building those lifelong bonds of trust and love through **hard** work. It's **really worth it**! As John's youth shared with you, it is their personal testimonies of ministry that will bring others to choir to do more than sing a song—to be ministered to with words of praise and lots of love.

As you encourage other youth to be involved in choir, here are some ways to use those testimonies in enrollment opportunities:

- Use your youth ensembles in older children's Sunday School classes to sing and tell what choir has meant to them.
- Use junior high vocal, instrumental, and bell groups to perform in older children's area in the spring before they are to join choir. Again, youth will share their testimonies about what choir means to them.
- Put youth testimonies in a brochure and mail them to the youth Sunday School roll (incoming youth from younger choir and those who will be your older group).
- If you have funds, send a youth mailout piece, in coordination with your youth minister, to a targeted area of homes in your surrounding area, zip code, or entire city to young people in those homes containing the age you are trying to reach. Information like this is available.
- Invite incoming youth from your oldest children's choir or junior high choir (if there is not a problem with groups meeting at the same time) to your rehearsal and let youth from your choir share testimonies about the importance of choir to them, and how your group looks forward to the contribution of these new members next year.
- Take a video of your tour and tape personal testimonies to show at choir enrollment day

in Sunday School departments as youth move to new classes or even mail copies to prospects with a cover letter; follow-up calls and/or visits by the director and a couple of young people.

Memories

(JL) So you see, building an effective youth choir ministry has many aspects and opportunities. Above all, be flexible with your ideas. If something doesn't work, change directions or try a different angle. Never be afraid to admit problems or even failure. As long as the youth realize you are striving to put the best possible things before them, they will love you for it and support your ministry.

Let us share a few memories of past youth choirs as a conclusion to this chapter. We do this, not to brag, but to encourage you in your efforts to serve as a youth choir director. We are not magicians who have pulled proverbial rabbits out of the hat. The best thing on our side has been time and determination. These traits are available to anyone who wants them badly enough.

(GW) I have found myself looking back through the years to the First Baptist Church of Siloam Springs, Arkansas, where I found myself under the tutelage of a man that I would, to this day, follow any-

where—without question. Why? Because of what he instilled in my life—to want other young people to know the joy of sharing Christ through music; to enjoy music as much as I have; to know that music is more than singing. It's the never-ending, never-tiring message of the great **I am**. One doesn't have to be a great soloist or a great instrumentalist to accomplish this. All God wants is **your best**. I see the faces of my own kids singing everywhere from the Air Force Academy chapel to the top of Stone Mountain, Georgia—every concert ending with "The Majesty and Glory of Your Name." I stop and think that the task to which God has called us—to direct a youth choir—seems insignificant to some, but to the youth we influence it is more than just directing a choir, it's a ministry of love, a life invested in someone very special. Each week I give a little part of my life away— my heart. I have a lot of heart to give, you see, because I carry in my life the heart of the one who taught me. Thanks, John Gardner. Preach on, John Link. May others who read our thoughts be once again moved to memories of past, present, and, hopefully, future memories that only a youth choir experience can give.

(JL) The dream I had at Ridgecrest™ Music Week has kept

my boat afloat for all these years. Bit by bit, I have been able to see dreams become reality. The following memories are special times within the life of a youth choir that should be cherished and used as motivational material for future choirs. They will hopefully spur you on to greater determination for making the best use of youth choir time.

The Memorable Lincoln Memorial

I nervously raised my hand to get the attention of the choir and realized they were as nervous as I was. It wasn't until then that I came to a full understanding of where I was. Peeking over the back row of the men's section were the steely eyes of Abraham Lincoln! Behind me was the beautiful Reflecting Pool and, true to its name, it reflected the Washington Monument in its waters. To the left, the long somber wall of the Vietnam War Memorial ran along the horizon. We were in Washington D.C., singing a concert on the steps of the Lincoln Memorial! A small group gathered in front of the pool as we began. The small electronic piano blared forth as we sang at the top of our lungs.

It was not the best choral concert ever sung by the choir, and the acoustics were not quite what you would want in a perfect set-

ting, but our hearts swelled with pride. It was a good sort of pride that included a mixture of patriotism, belief in God and church, and a healthy sense of satisfaction in knowing that these youth were singing in such a famous public place for God!

We did not have any converts and the crowd seemed to change with each song, but the feeling of being part of that scene will live on in the memories of our youth forever. We've sung hundreds of concerts in many different places, but none was quite so soul-stirring as the time when Honest Abe sang in the men's section!

Praising at PraiSing II

We quietly walked on stage: a famous stage that had held many famous people from all backgrounds and musical styles. The Grand Ole Opryhouse, Nashville, Tennessee, had never seemed to be quite this big from the audience. The 40-piece orchestra put the final touches on its tuning, and the one hundred tuxedos of the Centurymen made a beautiful background for the youth as they stood nervously with music in hand. As Buryl Red raised his baton to start the music, the crowd sat up expectantly.

No, this was not another dream: this was PraiSing II '91, the dedication of a new hymnal and the memory of a lifetime for our youth. All the long hours of rehearsal seemed to pale in importance as the youth sang the refrains from the old musical Good News. They were a part of Southern Baptist history, and they will become an important part of its future.

I couldn't stand being on the sideline any longer! Donning a youth choir shirt, I walked on stage, became part of the youth choir, and sang the songs with them. In that moment of singing as a youth choir member, a permanent bond grew between us. When they saw that I thought they were important enough to become one of them, a new level of relationship was born. And not just for them! My love for music, for Southern Baptists, for youth choirs, and for just plain singing was never greater.

Singing with Adrenaline

One year, our tour took us by Atlanta, Georgia, where the National Youth Minister's Conference was being held. After quite a bit of talking and convincing, we were given a spot on the program to sing one song while they were changing the stage. When we arrived at the convention center, we found, to our great surprise (or great dismay, depending on who you were!), that the Christian rock group Audio Adrenaline was performing immediately before we sang.

We were to be permitted to sit in on this short concert, sing our song, then leave—we thought! It turned out that Audio Adrenaline had a little too much juice and blew out the sound system for the conference. Not knowing the predicament, we were lining up on stage when a frantic young lady came up to apologize and to ask us to wait until the sound was restored.

Never being one to slap opportunity in the face, I told her that we would be happy to "entertain" until the sound system was fixed. I was very grateful that many of our songs could be done a cappella. They graciously agreed since they had no other choice, and we began our "one song." After about 30 minutes, the sound system was restored and the program went on, but what an impromptu concert we were able to have. We sang longer than Audio Adrenaline! I have always wanted to thank them for "warming up" the conference for us! In the midst of this, I was amazed at how all styles of music were equally appreciated and loved.

Even When Things Don't Go Right!

The old rattletrap bus shook uneasily as I turned onto the interstate. Things seemed to be falling apart faster than the old bus that I navigated down the road! One simple noon-day concert had turned into a nightmare! Looking back through the rearview mirror, I saw the worried faces of 15 youth. How could I do a concert with just 15 people!

It all started with an invitation to present a special concert for a convention in downtown Nashville. What seemed to be a perfect opportunity to sing turned to chaos when the public school threatened the youth with zeroes for each class they missed for the concert, even with permission from their parents! The choir had quickly dwindled from 50 to 15. Seven sopranos, four altos, three basses, and one tenor looked to the front of the bus for encouragement and enthusiasm. Maybe I could pick someone up along the way with those qualities!

We walked into the one-hundred seat choir loft without a word. As I turned to give some last-minute directions to the choir, a wonderful transformation took place. Upon each of their faces I saw enthusiasm—unbridled enthusiasm! They were excited about what they were going to do, about who they were, and about the message they had to give. Regardless of their number, they were about to sing. They drew confidence and encouragement

from past concerts and knew they could do it again, even in their diminutive numbers!

I brought them out of the choir loft and stood them on the pulpit steps. Things seemed a little less threatening there. Then, to my surprise, they sang with the enthusiasm of a one-hundred voice choir. After the concert we had a question and answer time. When asked how they could sing with such confidence, they answered that they knew no other way. Singing in choir had become an enthusiastic experience for them, regardless of the number of singers. I tried, in vain, to figure out some way to take credit for that answer, but the truth was simply that they were youth, with unlimited enthusiasm for life. Never underestimate youth!

The Last Concert

Every choir tour has its last concert and every last concert seems to be a special one. It's a culmination of every moment spent in preparation during the previous seven months. Every song is memorized, every drama polished; it's not going to get better than this! Emotions are at a high tide and the youth are focused. Oh, to have them poised like this every time they sing!

Then, to a smaller group, this concert is a conclusion of six years of growing and learning in youth choir. This group of seniors is always very special to me. Like captains on a sports team, they have taken the leadership role in choir and have provided an example for all the others. No one will match their enthusiasm during this last concert.

As each song slips by, the mood of the choir becomes more intense and emotions start to flow. Most are able to channel it into the music, but there are always a few who can't control the tears. As I direct each song, the youth seem to mature before my eyes. They become singers with a message, and they have a special motive for sharing that message with others. I wouldn't trade these moments for any college or professional choir around. These are my kids and, through the long hours of practice and concerts, they have finally reached a special goal. With a combined spirit of praise for our Lord, they are now giving their all in song, and they are enjoying it as much as I have enjoyed sharing it with them.

You see, the final key to having a successful youth choir is to enjoy it. Your enthusiasm is infectious and will, in the end, shine from their own faces like a mirror, reflecting your own feelings. Your love for the youth, for the music they sing and for the message they give, will turn a good choir into a great choir.

The final song begins and with one heart they lift up the words of the old hymn:

"Finish, then, Thy new creation;
Pure and spotless let us be;
Let us see Thy great salvation
Perfectly restored in Thee:
Changed from glory into glory,
Till in heaven we take our place,
'Till we cast our crowns before
    Thee,
Lost in wonder, love, and praise."[1]

The concert ends, and I can never tell whether a little of me is taken away into their hearts or a little of each one of the hearts of the youth have been added to mine. Perhaps it's a bit of both. This is why I continue to strive for excellence each year in youth choir. To see youth be "lost in wonder, love, and praise" gives me a hope for the future and a satisfaction of the past. Their lives, and mine, will never be quite the same.

Take the challenge of youth choir and embrace it wholly! Spend the time and energy it requires to make it successful. Then, reap the wonderful benefits in store for you. It has been the most satisfying challenge in my music ministry. May your quest for youth choir be no less!

[1]Charles Wesley, "Love Divine, All Loves Excelling."

CHAPTER 11

Where Do We Go From Here?

by Gerald Ware

As new youth consultants, this section of the book is dedicated to our vision for Southern Baptist youth choirs.

**Looking Ahead—
Our Dreams for the Future**

As a new millennium approaches, so does a new day in the youth choir area of the Southern Baptist Convention. As contract youth yusic consultants for the Baptist Sunday School Board, John and I are excited about developing innovative and practical means by which youth choir work can become a vibrant ministry in every church in our Convention. The key is that one person—**you**—has the desire, love, and willingness to invest time and energy in the lives of young people. We have already expressed our thoughts and ideas in several key areas that *will* work for you. Take the concept and apply it to your individual goal for your youth choir. You are not alone! Through a little organizational effort, you can surround yourself with a team of parents who will operate your choir smoothly and effectively. If you lack training but have the willingness to learn, here are some resources available to you *now*:

• ***Church Musician Today***. A monthly magazine published by the Baptist Sunday School Board. This magazine provides new and fresh ideas to music ministers in all facets of their ministry.

• **Glorieta™ and Ridgecrest™ Music Weeks**. Here is a wonderful opportunity to "get away" and enjoy God's handiwork while at the same time attending a smorgasbord of classes on youth choirs. There are music reading sessions, premiers of new musicals, and an afternoon round-table discussion and share time where ideas (what's working, what's not, and how can we do things better) are exchanged. Don't forget your most valuable resource while attending Music Week—other ministers of music.

• **State and regional music workshops through your state music office:** These are like a mini-Glorieta™ or Ridgecrest™ condensed into an intensive two–day conference, utilizing people from your state, as well as neighboring states, in a variety of training opportunities. Call your state music office or look for information in the mail for date, time, and place.

• **State youth music camps:** Your state may already be doing this (excellent training opportunities for your youth and youth choir director).

• Encourage your state music department and associational director of missions and associational music director to **use choirs that have participated in state or associational youth choir festivals to sing in various statewide meetings**. This is a great platform to encourage youth choirs and to give them a goal to shoot for. Vocal ensembles, instrumental groups, soloists, and bell choirs could also be used.

• *Youth Cue* **magazine** is full of great ideas and information about successful youth choirs. A must to order!

• **Music Ministries Department, Baptist Sunday School Board**: Conctact the Music Ministries Department of the Baptist Sunday School Board for details about the youth music ministry consultant program. Here are our **DREAMS** for the future:

  1. **Regional Youth Choir Celebrations/Festivals**. What is the key? *One* person— *you*—willing to invest time and energy in seeing a regional festival grow. One church with 2 choirs to 11 churches and 16 groups in 2 years (633 people) isn't bad, folks! It took one person with a desire to see it happen and succeed! You say, "I don't know how?!" A notebook on the concept—where to begin, how to organize such an undertaking, with detailed

sample letters, and so forth—is available from the Music Ministries Department. Follow each step, enlisting the help of a team in your area or state. *You will reach every church in your state with just a few people leading this effort!* You will succeed with a little organization and coordinated effort. We had 633 at our regional youth choir celebration in February 1997 (76 were nonparticipants). I was contacted by 2 other large churches in our area that heard about our success and said they would participate next year with 3 more choirs (200 more youth). We will be reaching 1000 youth in our region by the year 2000. I don't have to explain to you how festivals/celebrations can breed excitement. The key is *you!*

2. State youth choir and/or orchestra in every state.

3. Internet access for Genevox Music Group, and other publishers to provide immediate access to new music with 30–second spots (music and sound). If the listener likes the music, they can order directly from the publisher. By doing this, the publisher can save money on printing and mail.

4. Tape youth choir classes at Glorieta™ and Ridgecrest™ (audio) and make them available on the Internet. By the year 2000, we may have the technology for access to video capability over the Internet. For a nominal fee, classes could be accessed from both Glorieta™ and Ridgecrest™.

5. Provide access to all national and state youth choir training opportunities with schedule of subject matter to be taught. You might even be able to enroll for the conference by computer and send all registration information and fees over the Internet without leaving your office.

6. Discussion/conference call with selected ministers of music over the Internet. Conference leader could Fax or E-mail material, or send CD with all information in your own personal notebook before the conference.

7. Current events and ideas (state and national) on programs, socials, and so forth, at your fingertips, using Southern Baptist Convention as filter—put all ideas on the Internet.

8. Electronic newsletter/youth choir magazine with important events of state and Southern Baptist Convention youth choir work.

9. Take a national Southern Baptist youth choir and orchestra on an overseas music/mission trip every five years. This would be an auditioned group made up of the Convention's most talented youth.

10. The Baptist General Convention of Texas state music office, for example, has moved to the regional concept in most everything they do. Regional workshops, rather than associational, combine the resources of several associations, making it possible to do more for the dollar. The concept is growing stronger and getting larger every year. Our ideas and ways of reaching thousands more young people in the area of youth choir is limited only by our lack of vision and dreams.

I have shared a few of my **DREAMS** with you. What is your dream for reaching young people through music? Come on—let's dream together and think **big**!

APPENDIX

CHAPTER 3

Sample Letter to Guest

Sample Member Letter

Dear Rebecca:

What a joy and privilege to have you visit the best junior high choir anywhere!

I hope you enjoyed the fellowship and rehearsal experience last Sunday. Our activities are many. In addition to our regular Sunday afternoon rehearsals, we sing in our Sunday evening service once a month, have socials every six to seven weeks, make a lot of new friends, participate in a regional choir festival in February, and have two fundraising activities to help defray the cost of tour.

This year our tour will be June 2-8, and we plan to go to Florida. We hope you felt a warm welcome to our choir. We want you to visit us again SOON!

Dear Niki:

Just a note to let you know how happy I was to see you bring Rebecca to choir last Sunday. I get so EXCITED to see our choir members bringing their friends with them. Sharing Christ with a friend is one of the most IMPORTANT things you can do. There are many young people who need to get involved in church.

Thank you for setting an example of LEADERSHIP for our choir members in reaching out to other youth in our area. I am so PROUD of YOU!

CHAPTER 4

- **"Be Still"** (Two-part), by Hank Beebe, Hindon Publications
- **"Chant and Jubilation,"** SA(T)B, by Hal Hopson, Harold Flammer, Inc.
- **"Come, Christians, Join to Sing"** (Unison or two-part), by Kay Hawkes, Goodyear, Chapel Hill Music, Inc.
- **"I Will Rejoice"** (Two-part), arranged by Mark Hayes, Word Music
- **"Prayer for Guidance"** (Unison or two-part) by Allen Pote, Hinshaw Music Inc.
- **"Sing Ye Joyfully"** (Two-part), by Besig, GlorySound
- **"Alleluia! Hear the Sound"** (SAB), arrranged by Mike Paslay, Hinshaw Music Inc.
- **"Brighten My Soul with Sunshine"** (SAB), by Eilers, Hal Leonard Publishing Corp.
- **"Gloria"** (SAB), by Linda Spevacek, Jenson Publications, Inc.
- **"It Is a Good Thing to Give Thanks"** (SAB), by Eugene Butler, Agape
- **"Praise the Lord"** (SATB), arranged by Hal Hopson, Harold Flammer

- **"A Mighty Fortress Is Our God"** (SATB), aranged by Mark Hayes, Hal Leonard
- **"Amazing Grace / Kum Ba Yah"** (SATB), arranged by Beery/ Musser, Harold Flammer, Inc.
- **"Clap Your Hands"** (SATB), by Mary McDonald, Purifoy Publishing
- **"Elijah Rock"** (SSATB), arranged by Jester Hairston, Bourme Co.
- **"I Surrender All"** (SATB), arranged by Mark Hayes, GlorySound
- **"If I Have My Ticket"** (SATB), arranged by Donald Moore, CPP Belwin
- **"Let the Redeemed of the Lord Say So!"** (SATB), by Eugene Butler; Hinshaw Music Inc.
- **"Love, As Christ Would Love"** (SATB), by Bob Burroughs, Hinshaw Music Inc.
- **"On the Third Day"** (SATB), by Allen Pote; Hope Publishing Co.
- **"Washed in the Blood of the Lamb"** (SATB), arranged by Paul Ferrin, Word Music

CHAPTER 6

Sample Letter

Dear Junior High Parents:

Several years ago we started our Junior High Choir Parent Support Group. Each year over 50 of our parents commit themselves in various ways to help with choir activities—either weekly, monthly, or once a year. Whether your child shows it or not, he/she needs your support and does apreciate your involvement in the youth activities.

Please consider the following opportunities to serve, complete the form, and return it to my office by [date]. A personal goal: 106 youth enrolled in choir our first day. That usually reflects 70-75 percent of our enrollment for the year (117 enrolled in choir last year). I think 125 this year is a realistic goal. We have the best witnessing tool at our fingertips—your child!

I still dream of filling the choir loft with our youth. It can be done with your encouragement and your child's enthusiasm and willingness to give whatever talent he or she has to the glory of God.

Thank you for your help as we work together to train and lead our youth toward a closer relationship with God, and as we learn that true Christian love means to share it with others!

Sincerely yours,

FORM 2

JUNIOR HIGH CHOIR PARENTS SUPPORT GROUP

If you are willing to serve on the Junior High Choir Parents Support Group, please indicate the area where you would like to serve. If both parents wish to serve, indicate this also.

❏ Personnel/Membership—Assisting in the membership of each group; calling absentees every week; counseling when necessary. Attendance requirement: one Sunday per month (7 teams needed).

❏ Social—Assisting in the planning of all social activities. Attendance required only at social functions. If you drive the church van, you will need to provide your name and driver's license number to the church office.

❏ Administrative—Records, typing, seating, room temperature, money, room arrangement, and so forth. Attendance required once each week and at any "special" concert and Sunday evening service when the choir sings.

❏ Transportation—Provide transportation once each week (if necessary) to any youth who needs a ride.

❏ Miscellaneous—As needed, provide assistance for particular events or functions of the choir, perhaps only once a year.

❏ Publicity–Assist director in publicizing choir activities (Pancake Day, car wash, and home concert) through posters and other creative means.

❏ Choir Uniforms—Assist director in selection of choir uniform for the year, securing material with information on cost, and so forth. Also, enlist workers to assist with fitting, ordering, collection of payment, and distribution of uniforms.

❏ Rehearsal Assistants—Assist director each week in channeling the energy of the choir in the same direction by helping youth find music, by singing in sections, and by praising them for their hard work.

❏ Video—Be available to go on tour June 2–8 to make video of tour. Video will need to be no more than five minutes in length to show at home concert. Good audio track of choir singing or Christian artist can be used for background music. Work closely with director on this venture.

Signed:_____

Address:_____

_____

Home Phone: (_____)_____ Work Phone:(_____)_____

Your Child's Name:_____

FORM 3

JUNIOR HIGH CHOIR OFFICER
PSG COMMITTEE ASSIGNMENTS

(PSG) OFFICER (JUNIOR HIGH) COCHAIRMAN

Personnel/Membership (2)

Social (1)

Administrative (1)

Transportation (2)

Miscellaneous (1)

Publicity (2)

Rehearsal Helpers (2)

Choir Uniforms (1)

[President serves as cochair (1); Vice President serves as cochair (2)]

Video Director—serves on each committee

Choir director—serves on each committee

FORM 4

DUTIES OF JUNIOR HIGH CHOIR OFFICERS

PRESIDENT
1. Executive officer of the choir and ex officio member of all committees.
2. Preside at the general business meetings.
3. Appoint committees, when needed, after talking with director.
4. Work with music director in providing leadership and stimulating interest among the choir members.
5. Work closely with Parent Support Group cochairpersons in helping involve Parent Support Groups and their functions.
6. President and choir officers will be among the governing body concerning decisions about choir members who are in trouble (borderline) with attendance requirements, and so forth.
7. At the end of each rehearsal, president will introduce new members and visitors.

VICE PRESIDENT
1. Chairman of the membership committee, which will be composed of the group leaders.
2. Work closely with the Parent Support Group personnel/ membership committee in assisting with the ministry of this parent support group.
3. Work closely with the ministries chairman in helping meet needs of all choir members and the choir in general.
4. At the end of rehearsal, present an attendance report.

LIBRARIANS (2)
1. Prepare folders and have copies of all music in ready for each rehearsal.
2. Work closely with the administrative committee chairman in assisting with room setup and collection of music after each rehearsal.
3. Assist with distribution of music during rehearsal.
4. For new members or visitors, make certain they are welcomed and have a music folder.

GROUP LEADERS
(2 Girls, 2 Boys)
1. Work closely with the vice vresident and parent personnel/ membership committee chairman in enlistment of new members.
2. Assist ministries chairman, vice president, and parent personnel/membership committee

chairman in learning of any
problems choir members may
be having which might require
help (illness, death in family, and
so forth).
3. Maintain an accurate record of
absences (and excuses) of everyone in assigned group. These will
be discussed at a quarterly
meeting.
4. Where there is a shortage of
music, help those in assigned
section in sharing with those
who are without music.
5. Help keep choir informed of
special dates and activities.

SOCIAL COMMITTEE
(6 members)
1. The social committee will be
composed of two members from
each grade. The ninth grader
with the most votes will be
chairman of this group.
2. Work closely with the Parent
Support Group social committee chairperson and committee
in planning social events, banquets, parties.
3. Organize choir members so that
everyone assists throughout the
year with different social functions.
4. If the choir will be charged a fee
for a social, the committee will
inform the choir president several weeks before the function,
so that adequate publicity may
be planned and provided.

HISTORIAN (2)
1. Maintain an accurate record of
all group activities.
2. Work closely with the social
committee in knowing about
plans and in planning ahead for
film needed. (Note: Music budget will pay for film and developing costs.) Also, inform video
chairman of PSG to see if his
group can make a video of
socials, if time allows, in addition
to choir tour.
3. Take pictures and write articles
about the choir events. Also, col-
lect newspaper clippings, and so
forth, for a scrapbook.

MINISTRIES CHAIRMAN
1. The ministries chairman will
maintain close contact with
choir members, group leaders,
and Parent Support Group per-
sonnel/membership committee
in the areas of ministry for the
choir.
2. If there is a death of an immediate family member or illness of
a choir member, the ministries
chairman will send a card to that
choir member.
3. The ministries chairman should
always make visitors and new
members feel welcome.
4. Make a quarterly report at officers' meetings on accomplish-
ments or plans to better minister
to choir.

CHAPTER 8

PROGRAM INFORMATION GUIDE

1. Name of organization or group

   _____

   Telephone number (_____)_____
2. Contact person _____

   Home phone (____ ___)_____

   Work phone (_____)_____
3. Location of concert (with driving instructions)

   _____

   _____

   _____

   _____
4. Time of program_____ Length of program _____
5. Piano: YES_____ NO_____
6. PA system:

   YES_____ *(specify number of microphones needed)*

   NO_____ *(will need 6-foot table for sound board with electrical outlets nearby)*
7. Meal provided: YES_____ NO_____
8. If location is some distance away, could host help with gasoline expenses?

   YES____*(Cost of van = 30 cents per mile for van; 10 cents per mile for trailer.*

   Usually requires three vans.)

   NO_____
9. Where does group perform?

   Fellowship Hall____

   Sanctuary____

   Other (Specify)_____

   Through which doors does group enter?

   _____
10. What should group wear?

    _____

    _____

Thanks again for your ministry—so vital to reaching our community and beyond!

CHAPTER 9

Radio Publicity Release

10 Second Spot

The 110-voice Junior High Choir from First Baptist Church, Richardson, Texas, will appear in concert (day, date), at (time), in (location). Admission is free and the public is cordially invited.

30 Second Spot

The Junior High Choir of First Baptist Church, Richardson, Texas, is presenting a concert (day, date), at (time), in (location). The choir is composed of 120 members, of which 110 are on a 7-day tour of Florida, Mississippi, and Louisiana. The choir will present a variety of sacred music—from the classics to contemporary style. Vocal and instrumental ensembles, handbell choir, and a drama team are all part of this free concert. The public is cordially invited.

Newspaper Sample

(Newspaper Name)
(Address)
Attn: Religion Editor
Dear Editor:

Classic, contemporary, and gospel music at its best will be the fare of the evening (day, date), at (time) at (location) in (city) with the Junior High Choir from First Baptist Church, Richardson, Texas. This choir is composed of 120 members, 110 of which are on a 7-day tour of Florida, Mississippi, and Louisiana.

Please consider this a personal invitation to you and your family to attend this exciting concert and to ask you to share the concert information in your public service announcements and community religion section for the week of May 26-31.

Enclosed you will find one black-and-white glossy photo to use in advertising the concert—(day, date, time).

Thank you for your assistance.

Radio and Television Publicity

(Radio or Television Name)
(Address)
Attention: Public Service Director
Dear Director:

Classic, contemporary, and gospel music at its best will be the fare of the evening (day, date), at (time) at (location) in (city), with the Junior High Choir, First Baptist Church, Richardson, Texas. The choir is composed of 120 members, of which 110 are on a 7-day tour of Florida, Mississippi, and Louisiana.

Please consider this a personal invitation to you and your family to attend this exciting concert and to ask you to share the concert information in your public service announcements and community religion section for the week of May 26-31.

Thank you for your assistance.

> *Publicity suggestions may or may not be followed, but for the church that has never taken the initiative to publicize a concert, the above information will be helpful.*
